MW00964476

TLC
kitchen

TLC

kitchen

120 timeless recipes from our family to yours

Includes recipes from the stars of your favorite TLC series

www.parragon.com/lovefood

LOVE FOOD is an imprint of Parragon Books Ltd

LOVE FOOD and the accompanying heart device is a registered trademark of Parragon Books Ltd in the USA, the UK, Australia, India and the EU.

Parragon, Inc.
440 Park Avenue South
13th Floor
New York
NY10016
USA

Busy families need simple and easy solutions. This cookbook features delicious, easy-to-make recipes from a variety of chefs, including some of the stars of TLC's most popular series. From light bites to hearty meals and sweet treats, there is something for everyone.

- Learn how to prepare a deeply delicious Lemon Capellini by **Randy Fenoli** of *Say Yes to the Dress*

- Create decadent cupcakes courtesy of **Katherine and Sophie** from *DC Cupcakes*

- Create budget-conscious family meals from our very own **Mama June** from *Here Comes Honey Boo Boo*

- Whip up a moist and rich Red Velvet Cake, with a recipe from **Marissa Lopez** the Season Two winner from *Next Great Baker*

- Treat yourself to a Marinated Skirt Steak, a favorite of **Jen Arnold and Bill Klein** from the *The Little Couple*

- Indulge in a Chocolate-and-Vanilla Ice Cream Cake with a recipe created by **Buddy Valastro** from *Cake Boss*

Whether you're a beginner or advanced cook, we're sure you'll find a recipe inside that will soon become your own signature dish.

breakfast *and* brunch

cranberry-orange scones

makes 6 scones

Randy Fenoli
Say Yes to the Dress and *Randy To The Rescue*

PREP TIME: 10 minutes
COOK TIME: 15 minutes

2 cups unbleached
all-purpose flour

1 tbsp baking powder

5–6 tbsp sugar

$\frac{1}{2}$ tsp salt

1 tsp orange zest

5 tbsp cold unsalted butter,
cut into $\frac{1}{4}$-inch cubes

1 cup fresh or frozen (slightly
thawed) cranberries

1 cup heavy cream, plus more
for brushing

raw sugar, for sprinkling

cooking spray

Preheat oven to 425°F.

In a large bowl stir in flour, baking powder, sugar, salt and orange zest.

Mix in butter with fingertips until the consistency of coarse meal with a few slightly larger butter lumps.

Stir in cranberries and cream.

On a floured surface, form into a ball and pat into an 8-inch circle, about $\frac{3}{4}$-inch thick.

Brush top and sides with cream and sprinkle generously with raw sugar.

Cut into 8 triangles (like you would slice a pie).

Spray a baking sheet lightly with cooking spray, and wipe off any excess with a paper towel.

Bake for 12-15 minutes until lightly golden.

Resist eating them immediately. Let them rest about 10 minutes to firm up. Enjoy!

low-fat blueberry muffins

makes 12 muffins

PREP TIME: 15 minutes
COOK TIME: 25 minutes

²/₃ cups all-purpose flour
1 tsp baking soda
¹/₄ tsp salt
1 tsp ground allspice
1 cup superfine sugar
3 large egg whites
3 tbsp low-fat margarine, melted
²/₃ cup thick low-fat plain yogurt
or blueberry-flavored yogurt
1 tsp vanilla extract
3 oz fresh blueberries

Preheat the oven to 375°F. Line a 12-well muffin pan with paper liners.

Sift the flour, baking soda, salt and half of the allspice into a large mixing bowl. Add half of the sugar and mix together well.

In a separate bowl, whisk the egg whites together. Add the margarine, yogurt and vanilla extract and mix together well, then stir in the blueberries until thoroughly mixed.

Add the fruit mixture to the dry ingredients, then gently stir until just combined. Do not overstir—it is fine for it to be a little lumpy.

Divide the mixture evenly between the paper liners and fill about two-thirds full. Mix the remaining sugar with the remaining allspice and sprinkle over the muffins.

Bake in the preheated oven for 25 minutes, or until a toothpick inserted in the middle comes out clean. Remove the muffins from the oven.

Let cool or serve warm.

eggs benedict

makes 6 servings

PREP TIME: 10 minutes
COOK TIME: 15 minutes

Hollandaise sauce
2 sticks (16 tbsp) unsalted butter
5 large egg yolks
2 tbsp fresh lemon juice
cayenne pepper
salt

6 English muffins, halved
butter, for brushing
6 slices cooked ham
1 tbsp white-wine vinegar
salt
12 very fresh large eggs

To make the hollandaise sauce, melt the butter in a small saucepan over a medium heat, and keep over a very low heat until required. Put the egg yolks and lemon juice into a medium stainless-steel bowl. Place over a saucepan of gently simmering water, making sure that the bowl does not touch the water. Whisk constantly until the mixture thickens and is very warm to the touch.

Remove from the heat and very slowly drizzle in the melted butter, whisking constantly until it has all been incorporated. The mixture can be thinned with a tablespoon of hot water, if liked. Whisk in cayenne pepper and salt to taste. Cover with foil and set aside in a warm place.

Put the muffin halves on a baking sheet and toast under the broiler until golden, then brush with butter. Cut the ham slices in half and place 1 piece on each muffin half. Remove from the heat and keep warm in a low oven.

Pour 3 inches of water into a large, deep frying pan, add the vinegar and some salt and bring to simmering point. Crack the eggs into the simmering water and cook for 2 minutes, until heated through but still soft. Remove with a slotted spoon and place 1 egg on each muffin half. Spoon over the warm hollandaise sauce and serve immediately.

breakfast and brunch

cheese blintzes with strawberry sauce

makes 8–10 blintzes

PREP TIME: 10 minutes
COOK TIME: 50 minutes, plus
1-2 hours chilling time

Crêpes

1 cup whole milk
¼ cup cold water
2 large eggs
1 cup all-purpose flour
pinch salt
1 tbsp sugar
3 tbsp vegetable oil
cooking spray

Filling

1½ cups ricotta cheese
½ cup (4 oz) cream cheese
3 tbsp confectioners' sugar, plus
more for dusting
1 tsp freshly grated lemon zest
1 large egg

Sauce

¾ cup strawberry preserves, or
any other fruit jam or jelly
¼ cup water

2 tbsp butter for browning, plus
more for greasing the pan

For the crêpes, pour the milk, water, eggs, flour, salt, sugar and vegetable oil in a blender. Blend the batter until it is very smooth. Refrigerate for 1 to 2 hours before making crêpes.

For the filling, combine the ricotta cheese, cream cheese, confectioners' sugar, lemon zest and egg in a blender and blend until smooth. Refrigerate.

For the sauce, add the preserves and water to a small saucepan over medium heat. Bring to a simmer, stirring, and turn off. Strain, if desired. Reserve.

Preheat oven to 400°F. To cook the crêpes, place an 8-inch nonstick skillet over medium heat; spray lightly with cooking spray. Pour in ¼ cup of batter into the center of the pan and tilt it around so the batter covers the bottom evenly.

Cook for about 1 minute, then flip with a spatula and cook the other side for 30 seconds. Transfer the crêpes to a plate, and continue until the batter is gone.

To make the blintzes, spoon about 2 tbsp of the cheese filling into the center bottom third of a crêpe. Fold the bottom up over the filling, fold in the sides, and roll to make a neat rectangular package.

When all the blintzes are filled and rolled, melt the butter in a nonstick skillet over medium heat. Brown the blintzes lightly on each side, starting with the seal side down.

Transfer them to a lightly buttered baking dish. Bake in the oven for 15 minutes. Let rest for 5 minutes before serving with the fruit sauce. Dust with confectioners' sugar, if desired.

quick ham-and-cheese omelet

makes 1 serving

PREP TIME: 5 minutes
COOK TIME: 5 minutes

2 extra-large eggs
salt and pepper

1 tsp butter
1 tsp vegetable oil
⅓ **cup chopped, cooked sliced ham**
½ **cup shredded Swiss, American, or cheddar cheese**
salt and pepper

Break the eggs into a bowl, season with salt and pepper, and lightly beat with a fork.

Heat a small omelet pan or nonstick skillet until hot and add the butter and oil, swirling to coat evenly. Pour in the egg mixture, tilting to spread, and cook for 5 seconds.

Use a spatula to draw in the edges of the omelet toward the center. Continue until most of the liquid is set.

Sprinkle the omelet with the ham and half of the cheese. Fold over one side to enclose the filling and sprinkle with the remaining cheese. Serve immediately.

tip You can use many different food combinations to replace the ham and cheese for special-occasion breakfasts—you could try sautéed morel mushrooms with asparagus tips, or, for the ultimate touch of luxury, some delicious smoked salmon.

corned beef hash

makes 6 servings

PREP TIME: 15 minutes
COOK TIME: 30 minutes

2 tbsp butter

1 tbsp vegetable oil

1½ lb cooked corned beef,
cut into small cubes

½ cup diced onion

1½ lb white potatoes, peeled,
cut into small cubes

salt and fresh ground black
pepper to taste

¼ tsp paprika

¼ tsp garlic powder

¼ cup diced green bell pepper,
or jalapeño if a spicier version
is desired

2 tbsp prepared roasted-tomato
salsa

1 tbsp freshly sliced chives

Add the butter, oil, corned beef and onions to a large, cold nonstick or well-seasoned cast-iron skillet. Turn heat to medium-low and cook, stirring occasionally, while you prepare the potatoes.

In a saucepan, boil the potatoes in salted water for about 5 to 7 minutes (depending on the size), until partially cooked but still very firm. Drain very well and add to the skillet along with the rest of the ingredients, except the chives.

Mix together thoroughly with the hot corned-beef mixture, and press down slightly with a spatula to flatten. Turn up the heat to medium. Every 10 minutes or so, turn the mixture over with a spatula to bring the crusty bottom up to the top. Do this several times until the mixture is well-browned. Take your time — the only real secret to great corned beef hash is to make sure it cooks long enough, so the potatoes are crisp-edged and the cubes of meat get nicely caramelized.

Taste for salt and pepper, and adjust if necessary. Transfer to plates, and top with poached eggs, if desired. Garnish with freshly chopped chives.

breakfast and brunch

apple-spiced oatmeal

serves 4

PREP TIME: 10 minutes
COOK TIME: 15 minutes

2$\frac{1}{2}$ cups milk or water

1 tsp salt

1$\frac{1}{4}$ cups old-fashioned rolled oats

2 large apples

$\frac{1}{2}$ tsp apple-pie spice

honey, to serve (optional)

Put the milk in a saucepan and bring to a boil. Add the salt and sprinkle in the oats, stirring continuously.

Place over low heat and let the oats simmer for 10 minutes, stirring occasionally.

Meanwhile, peel, halve, core and grate the apples. When the oatmeal is creamy and most of the liquid has evaporated, stir in the grated apple and apple-pie spice. Spoon into serving bowls and drizzle with the honey, if using.

tip   Stir in $\frac{1}{2}$ cup chopped walnuts just before serving for a deliciously crunchy oatmeal.

banana pancakes
with whipped maple butter

serves 4

PREP TIME: 15 minutes
COOK TIME: 10 minutes

1¼ cups all-purpose flour
1½ tsp baking powder
1 tbsp granulated sugar
pinch of salt
1 cup buttermilk
1 extra-large egg
2 tbsp melted butter, plus extra
for greasing
3 ripe bananas
finely grated zest of 1 small
orange

Maple butter
6 tbsp butter, room temperature
¼ cup maple syrup

Sift the flour, baking powder, sugar and salt into a bowl. Add the buttermilk, egg and butter and beat to a smooth batter. Mash 2 bananas and mix thoroughly into the batter with the orange zest. Let stand for 5 minutes.

Lightly grease a griddle pan or skillet and heat over medium heat. Spoon ¼ cup of batter into the pan and cook until bubbles appear on the surface.

Turn over with a spatula and cook the other side until golden-brown. Repeat this process using the remaining batter, while keeping the cooked pancakes warm.

For the maple butter, beat together the butter and maple syrup, beating until light and fluffy.

Slice the remaining banana and serve with the pancakes, with the maple butter spooned over the pancakes.

variation For a subtly different finish, replace the maple syrup in the butter with an equal quantity of a delicately flavored clear honey, such as orange blossom.

new orleans–style french toast

makes 4–6 servings

PREP TIME: 5 minutes

COOK TIME: 1 hour

5 large eggs

1 cup milk

½ cup heavy cream

pinch of salt

1 tbsp sugar

2 tsp vanilla extract

½ tsp cinnamon

⅛ tsp allspice

12 thick slices day-old French bread (use a regular-sized loaf, not the skinny baguette type)

6 tbsp butter, plus more as needed

Preheat oven to 375°F. In a large mixing bowl, whisk together the eggs, milk, cream, salt, sugar, vanilla extract, cinnamon and allspice. Soak the bread slices in the custard mixture for at least 20 minutes, or until completely saturated.

Melt a few tbsp butter in a large non-stick skillet over medium heat. Add the bread in batches and lightly brown, about 2 minutes per side. Don't cook too dark, as additional browning will occur in the oven.

Transfer to lightly buttered, foil-lined baking sheets, and bake for 10 minutes. After 10 minutes, remove, and turn each slice over. Put back in the oven for another 10 to 15 minutes, or until browned and the bread springs back slightly when tested with a finger. Serve immediately.

fact The thrifty French (who pride themselves on the short life of their bread) are believed to have invented French toast as a way of using up bread that is no longer fresh—the French name for this tasty morsel is *pain perdu,* or "lost bread."

sandwiches *and* snacks

Jen and Bill Klein
The Little Couple

This recipe is great for parties. It can feed a small army and is so easy to make.

jen's spoon taco

serves 8

■ ■ ■

PREP TIME: 10 minutes

COOK TIME: 40 minutes

1 (30 oz) bag of tortilla chips

2 cans (15–20 oz) meat chili (no beans)

16 slices, soft processed cheese (like Velveeta)

1 (20 oz) jar of salsa (you choose the heat)

1 cup shredded cheddar/taco cheese

2 or 3 finely sliced jalapeño peppers

½ cup finely chopped onion

2 cans (15–20oz) refried beans

Preheat oven to 450°F.

In a large deep-based baking tray, create your spoon taco layers. Here is a suggested order:

Start by creating a layer of tortilla chips that covers the bottom of the tray.

Then add a layer of meat chili.

After that, add a layer of the sliced cheese (evenly disperse the slices to best cover the whole tray).

After that, a layer of salsa can be added.

Then add another layer of chips.

Then add a layer of the shredded cheese.

Drop in ¾ of the jalapeño peppers and about all of the chopped onions over the salsa.

Then add a layer of the refried beans.

Then one more layer of chips.

Finally add one more layer of shredded cheese and the remaining jalapeños to add some color.

Cover your tray with foil and place in the oven and bake for 30 minutes. Remove the foil and bake for another 10 minutes to make the top crispy. Remove from the oven, grab a plate and dig in—be careful, it's hot!

deviled-crab ramekins

makes 4 servings

PREP TIME: 10 minutes
COOK TIME: 15 minutes

melted butter, for greasing
6 oz crabmeat (light and dark meat)
1 extra-large egg, beaten
¼ cup crème fraîche or sour cream
juice of 1 lime
1 tsp hot chili sauce
2 cups fresh white breadcrumbs
salt and pepper
¼ cup Parmesan cheese, finely grated
paprika, to garnish

To serve
lime wedges
salad greens
toasted whole-wheat bread

Preheat the oven to 400°F. Brush four (²/₃ cup) ramekins with butter and place on a baking sheet.

Mix the crabmeat with the egg, crème fraîche, lime juice and chili sauce. Stir in the breadcrumbs and season with salt and pepper.

Spoon the mixture into the prepared ramekins and sprinkle with the cheese. Bake in the preheated oven for about 15 minutes, until golden and bubbling.

Sprinkle with paprika and serve hot with lime wedges, salad greens and toast.

variation   For a richly decadent spin on this elegant appetizer, substitute heavy cream for the crème fraîche.

chicken fajitas

makes 4 servings

PREP TIME: 20 minutes, plus
2–3 hours chilling time
COOK TIME: about 10 minutes

3 tbsp olive oil, plus extra
for drizzling

3 tbsp maple syrup or honey

1 tbsp red-wine vinegar

2 garlic cloves, crushed

2 tsp dried oregano

1–2 tsp crushed red pepper
flakes

salt and pepper

4 boneless, skinless chicken
breasts

2 red bell peppers, seeded
and cut into 1-inch strips

8 tortillas, warmed

Place the oil, maple syrup, vinegar, garlic, oregano and crushed red pepper in a large, shallow dish or bowl, season with salt and pepper, and mix together.

Slice the chicken across the grain into 1-inch-thick slices. Toss in the marinade until well coated. Cover and chill in the refrigerator for 2–3 hours, turning occasionally.

Heat a grill pan or skillet until hot. Lift the chicken slices from the marinade with a slotted spoon, lay on the grill pan, and cook over medium-high heat for 3–4 minutes on each side, or until cooked through. Remove the chicken to a warm serving plate and keep warm.

Add the bell peppers, skin side down, to the pan and cook for 2 minutes on each side. Transfer to the serving plate. Serve with the warm tortillas to be used as wraps.

mustard-and-honey wings

makes 4 servings

PREP TIME: 10 minutes, plus 1 hour marinating time
COOK TIME: 10-15 minutes

8 chicken wings
fresh flat-leaf parsley sprigs, to garnish

Glaze
½ cup honey
¼ cup Dijon mustard
¼ cup whole-grain mustard
¼ cup white-wine vinegar
2 tbsp vegetable oil
salt and pepper

Using a sharp knife, make a few diagonal slashes in the chicken wings and place them in a large nonmetallic dish.

Mix together all the ingredients for the glaze in a small bowl.

Pour the glaze over the wings, turning until the wings are well coated. Cover with plastic wrap and let marinate in the refrigerator for at least 1 hour.

Preheat the broiler to high. Drain the chicken wings, reserving the marinade. Cook the chicken under the preheated broiler, turning frequently and basting with the reserved marinade, for 10–15 minutes, or until a fork can be inserted into the thickest part of the meat with ease and the juices run clear. A meat thermometer inserted into the thickest part of the meat, without touching the bone, should read 170°F.

Transfer to serving plates, garnish with parsley sprigs and serve.

roasted-vegetable and feta-cheese wraps

makes 4 servings

PREP TIME: 20 minutes
COOK TIME: 20 minutes

1 red onion, cut into eighths

1 red bell pepper, seeded and cut into eighths

1 small eggplant, sliced lengthwise and cut into eighths

1 zucchini, sliced lengthwise and cut into eighths

$^1/_4$ cup extra virgin olive oil

1 garlic clove crushed

salt and pepper

$^2/_3$ cup crumbled feta cheese

small bunch fresh mint, shredded

four (10-inch) sandwich wraps

Preheat the oven to 425°F. Mix together all of the vegetables, olive oil and garlic, season with salt and pepper, and spread in a single layer on a nonstick roasting pan. Roast for 15–20 minutes, or until golden and cooked through.

Remove from the oven and let cool. Once cool, mix in the feta and mint.

Preheat a nonstick skillet or grill pan until almost smoking, then toast the wraps one at a time on both sides for 10 seconds.

Divide the vegetable-and-feta mixture among the wraps, placing it along the middle of each wrap. Roll up the wrap, cut them in half, and serve.

variation To add some fresh peppery crunch to these delicious wraps, divide a handful of arugula or watercress among them before adding the roasted vegetables.

fish goujons with chili mayonnaise

makes 4 servings

PREP TIME: 10 minutes
COOK TIME: about 10 minutes

1 cup all-purpose flour
salt and pepper
3 large eggs
1 cup matzo meal
1 lb firm whitefish fillets,
cut into strips
peanut oil, for shallow-frying

Chili mayonnaise
2 tbsp sweet chili sauce
4–5 tbsp mayonnaise

Mix the flour with plenty of salt and pepper on a large flat plate.

Beat the eggs in a bowl.

Spread out the matzo meal on another flat plate.

Dip the fish pieces into the seasoned flour, then into the beaten egg and finally into the matzo meal, ensuring a generous coating.

Heat $1/2$ inch of oil in a nonstick skillet. Cook the fish pieces in batches for a few minutes, turning once, until golden and cooked through.

For the chili mayonnaise, put the chili sauce and mayonnaise in a bowl and beat together until combined.

Transfer the fish to warmed plates and serve with the chili mayonnaise on the side.

variation Try adding a tastebud-tingling 2 teaspoons of lime juice to the mayonnaise, whisking well to avoid curdling.

sandwiches and snacks

beef wraps with lime and honey

makes 4 servings

PREP TIME: 10 minutes, plus
20 minutes marinating time

COOK TIME: about 5 minutes

finely grated zest and juice
of 1 lime
1 tbsp honey
1 garlic clove, crushed
1 lb tenderloin steak
salt and pepper
oil, for brushing

¼ cup mayonnaise
4 large flour tortillas
1 red onion, thinly sliced
3-inch piece cucumber, sliced
into ribbons

Mix together the lime juice, honey and garlic in a bowl and add the steak. Cover and let marinate in the refrigerator for 20 minutes.

Remove the steak from the marinade and season with salt and pepper. Heat a heavy skillet or ridged grill pan and brush with oil. Add the steak to the skillet and cook, turning once, for 5–6 minutes, until golden-brown.

Remove the steak from the heat, let stand for 2 minutes, then cut into thin strips.

Mix together the mayonnaise and grated lime zest and spread over the tortillas. Sprinkle the onion over the mayonnaise mixture and add the steak strips and cucumber. Wrap the sides over and turn over one end. Serve.

variation Add some sliced mango to each wrap—it's the perfect exotic partner for lime and is the fruit of choice for complementing savory dishes.

tuna-and-tomato pita pockets

makes 4 servings

PREP TIME: 10 minutes

COOK TIME: no cooking

4 pieces pita bread

1 head butterhead lettuce, coarsely shredded

8 cherry tomatoes, halved

1 (12-oz) can chunk light tuna in oil, drained and flaked

½ cup mayonnaise

1 tsp finely grated lemon zest

2 tbsp lemon juice

3 tbsp chopped fresh chives

salt and pepper

Cut each pita in half and open them to make a pocket.

Divide the lettuce among the pitas, then add the tomatoes and tuna.

Put the mayonnaise, lemon zest, lemon juice and chives into a bowl and mix together. Season with salt and pepper and spoon over the pita filling to serve.

variation You could add any number of ingredients to these tasty pockets to vary the flavors—try feta cheese, chopped red bell peppers or pitted black olives.

sandwiches and snacks

crab cakes with tartar sauce

makes 6 cakes

PREP TIME: 10 minutes, plus
1 hour chilling time
COOK TIME: 10 minutes

Tartar sauce

1 cup mayonnaise

¼ cup sweet pickle relish

1 tbsp very finely chopped onion

1 tbsp chopped capers

1 tbsp chopped parsley

1½ tbsp freshly squeezed
lemon juice

dash of Worcestershire sauce

few drops of Tabasco sauce
(optional)

salt and pepper

1 extra-large egg, beaten

2 tbsp mayonnaise

½ tsp Dijon mustard

¼ tsp Worcestershire sauce

½ tsp Old Bay seasoning

¼ tsp salt, or to taste

pinch of cayenne pepper
(optional)

10 saltine crackers

1 lb fresh crabmeat

⅓–¾ cup plain breadcrumbs

1 tbsp vegetable oil

2 tbsp unsalted butter

salad greens and lemon wedges,
to serve

To make the tartar sauce, mix all the ingredients together in a bowl and season with salt and pepper to taste. Chill for at least 1 hour before serving.

Put the egg, mayonnaise, mustard, Worcestershire sauce, Old Bay seasoning, salt and cayenne pepper, if using, into a mixing bowl and whisk to combine. Crush the crackers into very fine crumbs, add to the bowl, and combine. Let rest for 5 minutes.

Gently fold in the crabmeat and mix to combine the ingredients. Try not to mash the crab any more than necessary. Cover and chill for at least 1 hour.

Sprinkle breadcrumbs over a large plate until lightly covered. Shape the crab mixture into 6 evenly sized cakes, about 1-inch thick, and place on the plate as they are formed. Lightly dust the tops of each cake with more breadcrumbs.

Heat the oil and butter in a large skillet over medium-high heat. When the foam from the butter begins to dissipate, carefully transfer each crab cake from the plate to the skillet.

Sauté the cakes for about 4 minutes per side, until golden-brown. Remove from the skillet, drain on paper towels, and serve with the tartar sauce, salad greens and lemon wedges.

salads *and* dressings

caesar salad

makes 4 servings

PREP TIME: 10 minutes
COOK TIME: about 10 minutes

½ cup olive oil

2 garlic cloves

5 slices white bread, crusts
removed, cut into ½-inch cubes

1 large egg

3 heads Romaine lettuce

2 tbsp lemon juice

salt and pepper

8 canned anchovy fillets, drained
and coarsely chopped

fresh Parmesan cheese shavings,
to serve

Heat ¼ cup of the oil in a heavy skillet. Add the garlic and bread and
cook, stirring frequently, for 4–5 minutes, until the bread is crisp
and golden.

Remove the croutons from the skillet with a slotted spoon and drain
on paper towels.

Meanwhile, bring a small saucepan of water to a boil. Add the egg and
cook for 1 minute, then remove from the pan and set aside.

Arrange the lettuce leaves in a bowl.

In a separate bowl, add the remaining oil and the lemon juice, season
with salt and pepper, and mix together.

Crack the egg into the dressing and beat to blend. Pour the dressing
over the lettuce and toss well.

Add the chopped anchovies and croutons, discarding the garlic,
and toss the salad again. Sprinkle with Parmesan cheese shavings
and serve.

salads and dressings

fresh potato salad

makes 4–6 servings

PREP TIME: 20 minutes
COOK TIME: 12 minutes

2 lbs small new potatoes,
unpeeled

16–18 cornichons or sweet
gherkins, halved diagonally,
or dill-pickle slices

2 tbsp finely chopped red onion

3 tbsp snipped chives

¼ tsp pepper

salt

Mustard vinaigrette

2 tsp Dijon mustard

1 tbsp red-wine vinegar

¼ tsp pepper

sea-salt flakes

¼ cup extra-virgin olive oil

Put the potatoes in a saucepan of lightly salted water and bring to a boil. Reduce the heat to medium and cook for 10–12 minutes, until tender. Drain, then return to the pan and let stand for a few minutes.

To make the mustard vinaigrette, combine the mustard, vinegar, pepper and a pinch of sea-salt flakes in a bowl, mixing well. Add the olive oil and beat until smooth and thickened.

Put the potatoes in a serving bowl and pour the dressing over them. Add the remaining ingredients and toss gently to mix. Let stand at room temperature for at least 30 minutes before serving.

variation For a creamy but tangy alternative dressing for this salad, mix together 2 teaspoons of Dijon mustard, 2 tablespoons of mayonnaise and 2 teaspoons of lemon juice and season to taste with pepper. Add a little extra-virgin olive oil if necessary to achieve the right consistency.

winter salad slaw

makes 4–6 servings

PREP TIME: 15 minutes

COOK TIME: no cooking

1½ cups finely shredded green cabbage

2 carrots, shredded

1 celery stalk, thinly sliced

3 scallions, thinly sliced

1 Red Delicious or Pink Lady apple

2 tbsp lime juice

2 tbsp toasted pumpkin seeds

Dressing

½ cup plain yogurt

2 tbsp mayonnaise

2 tbsp finely chopped parsley

salt and pepper

Put the cabbage, carrots, celery and scallions into a large bowl and mix together. Coarsely grate the apple and discard the core, then sprinkle with the lime juice and add to the vegetables.

To make the dressing, mix together the yogurt, mayonnaise and parsley, then season with salt and pepper.

Pour the dressing over the prepared vegetables and toss well to coat evenly. Sprinkle with the pumpkin seeds and serve cold.

variation   For a nuttier finish, sprinkle the finished salad with sunflower seeds or toasted pine nuts as an alternative to the toasted pumpkin seeds.

salads and dressings

salad niçoise

makes 4–6 servings

PREP TIME: 35 minutes

COOK TIME: 10 minutes

2 tuna steaks, about $^3/_4$-inch thick

olive oil, for brushing

salt and pepper

2$^1/_4$ cups trimmed green beans

store-bought garlic vinaigrette, to taste

2 hearts of lettuce, leaves separated

3 extra-large hard-boiled eggs, halved

2 tomatoes, cut into wedges

1 (2-oz) can anchovy fillets in oil, drained

$^1/_2$ cup Niçoise olives or Kalamata olives

Heat a ridged, cast-iron grill pan over high heat. Brush the tuna steaks with oil on one side, place oiled side down on the hot pan, and grill for 2 minutes.

Lightly brush the top side of the tuna steaks with a little more oil. Turn the tuna steaks over, then season with salt and pepper. Continue grilling for an additional 2 minutes for rare or up to 4 minutes for well-done. Let cool.

Meanwhile, bring a saucepan of lightly salted water to a boil. Add the beans to the pan and bring back to a boil, then boil for 3 minutes. Drain the beans and immediately transfer to a large bowl. Pour the garlic vinaigrette over the beans and stir together.

To serve, line a serving dish with lettuce leaves. Lift the beans out of the bowl, leaving the excess dressing behind, and pile them in the center of the dish. Break the tuna into large flakes and arrange it over the beans.

Arrange the hard-boiled eggs, tomatoes, anchovy fillets and olives on the dish. Drizzle with more vinaigrette, if required, and serve.

honey-and-mustard chicken pasta salad

makes 4 servings

PREP TIME: 25 minutes
COOK TIME: 20 minutes

Dressing
3 tbsp olive oil
1 tbsp sherry vinegar
2 tsp honey
1 tbsp fresh thyme leaves
salt and pepper

8 oz dried fusilli
2 tbsp olive oil
1 onion, thinly sliced
1 garlic clove, crushed
4 boneless, skinless chicken breasts (about 4 oz each), thinly sliced
2 tbsp whole-grain mustard
2 tbsp honey
10 cherry tomatoes, halved
handful of mizuna or arugula leaves
fresh thyme leaves, to garnish

To make the dressing, place all the ingredients, including salt and pepper to taste, in a small bowl and whisk together until well blended.

Bring a large, heavy saucepan of lightly salted water to a boil. Add the fusilli, bring back to a boil, and cook according to the package directions, until just tender but still firm to the bite.

Meanwhile, heat the oil in a large skillet. Add the onion and garlic and sauté for 5 minutes. Add the chicken and cook, stirring frequently, for 3–4 minutes. Stir the mustard and honey into the skillet and cook for an additional 2–3 minutes, until the chicken and onion are golden-brown and sticky. Check the chicken is tender and cooked through—when cut through with a knife, there should be no signs of pink.

Drain the pasta and transfer to a serving bowl. Pour the dressing over the pasta and toss well. Stir in the chicken and onion and let cool.

Gently stir the tomatoes and mizuna into the pasta. Serve garnished with thyme leaves.

avocado, feta and arugula salad

makes 4 servings

PREP TIME: 10 minutes
COOK TIME: 5 minutes

2 ripe avocados

4 cups arugula

1²/₃ cups crumbled feta cheese

Dressing

¹/₃ cup olive oil

2 tbsp white-wine vinegar

1 shallot, finely chopped

2 large ripe tomatoes, seeded
and diced

1 tbsp lemon juice

salt and pepper

Halve, pit, peel and slice the avocados and arrange on a serving dish with the arugula. Top with the cheese.

To make the dressing, put the oil and vinegar into a saucepan and gently heat, then add the shallot and cook, stirring, for 2–3 minutes, until soft. Add the tomatoes, lemon juice and sugar and gently heat, stirring, for 30 seconds.

Season the dressing with salt and pepper, then spoon it over the salad and serve immediately.

variation Lift this salad out of the ordinary with an extra-special dressing—puree together 1 cup hulled whole strawberries, ¹/₂ cup olive oil, ¹/₂ cup sunflower oil, then add a pinch of sugar, season with salt and pepper to taste, and spoon over the salad.

summer couscous salad

makes 4–6 servings

PREP TIME: 20 minutes, plus 10 minutes to absorb the water

COOK TIME: 15 minutes

2 cups couscous

½ tsp salt

2 cups warm water

1–2 tbsp olive oil

4 scallions, finely chopped or sliced

1 bunch fresh mint, finely chopped

1 bunch fresh flat-leaf parsley, finely chopped

1 bunch fresh cilantro, finely chopped

1 tbsp butter

½ preserved lemon, finely chopped

Preheat the oven to 350°F. Put the couscous into an ovenproof dish. Stir the salt into the water and then pour over the couscous. Cover and let the couscous absorb the water according to the package directions.

Drizzle the oil over the couscous. Using your fingers, rub the oil into the grains to break up the lumps and aerate them. Toss in the scallions and half the herbs. Dot the surface with the butter and cover with a piece of aluminum foil or wet wax paper. Bake in the preheated oven for about 15 minutes to heat through.

Fluff up the grains with a fork and transfer the couscous to a serving dish. Toss the remaining herbs into the couscous and sprinkle the preserved lemon over the top. Serve.

tip If you don't have any preserved lemons in your pantry, make this quick and easy substitute—thinly slice 1 lemon, add to a skillet with 1 tablespoon of olive oil, 1 teaspoon of sugar and a little salt and gently sauté over medium heat until very soft.

cobb salad

makes 4 servings

PREP TIME: 15 minutes
COOK TIME: about 10 minutes

8 slices bacon

4 large handfuls mixed salad leaves, torn into bite-sized pieces

3 hard-boiled eggs, peeled and chopped

1 lb cooked chicken, diced

2 avocados, peeled, pitted and diced

6$\frac{1}{2}$ oz cherry tomatoes, halved

4 oz Roquefort cheese, crumbled

Dressing

$\frac{1}{2}$ tsp Dijon mustard

$\frac{1}{4}$ cup red-wine vinegar

1 tsp Worcestershire sauce

1 garlic clove, crushed into a paste

$\frac{1}{4}$ tsp salt

$\frac{1}{4}$ tsp pepper

6 tbsp olive oil

Put the bacon in a frying pan over a medium-high heat, cook until crisp (about 8–10 minutes), then drain on paper towels. When it is cool enough to handle, crumble and set aside.

Make a bed of salad leaves in 4 shallow bowls. Arrange the eggs, bacon, chicken, avocados, tomatoes and cheese in rows on top of the lettuce, covering the surface completely.

To make the dressing, whisk together the mustard, vinegar, Worcestershire sauce, garlic, salt and pepper.

Slowly drizzle in the oil, whisking constantly. Drizzle the dressing evenly over the salad, and serve immediately.

fact   Robert Cobb, of the original Brown Derby restaurant in Hollywood, is credited with the invention of this delicious, high-protein salad.

salads and dressings

red salad with beets and radish

makes 4 servings

PREP TIME: 10 minutes

COOK TIME: no cooking

8 small cooked beets, quartered

1 small red onion, cut into thin wedges

1 bunch radishes, sliced

2 tbsp chopped fresh mint

flatbread, to serve

Dressing

⅓ cup extra-virgin olive oil

1 tbsp whole-grain mustard

1 tbsp balsamic vinegar

1 tbsp lemon juice

2 tsp honey

salt and pepper

Toss together the beets, onion and radishes and stir in half the mint. Arrange on four serving plates.

To make the dressing, put the oil, mustard, vinegar, lemon juice and honey into a screw-top jar and shake well to mix. Season with salt and pepper.

Spoon the dressing over the salad and sprinkle the remaining mint on top. Serve immediately with flatbread.

tip If you feel like adding some leaves to this salad, stick with the red theme and make a bed of shredded crunchy radicchio on each plate before adding the other ingredients.

soups *and* stews

quick tomato soup

makes 4 servings

PREP TIME: 5 minutes
COOK TIME: 10–15 minutes

2 tbsp olive oil

1 large onion, chopped

1 (14.5-oz) can peeled plum tomatoes

1 $\frac{1}{4}$ cups chicken stock or vegetable stock

1 tbsp tomato paste

1 tsp hot chili sauce

handful of fresh basil leaves

salt and pepper

Heat the oil in a large saucepan over medium heat, add the onion and sauté for 4–5 minutes, stirring, until soft.

Add the tomatoes and their juices, stock, tomato paste, chili sauce and half of the basil leaves.

Purée in a blender until smooth, then transfer to the pan.

Stir the soup over medium heat until just boiling, then season with salt and pepper.

Serve the soup in warm serving bowls, garnished with the remaining basil leaves.

tip If your preference is for less rather than more spice, replace the hot chili sauce with 2 teaspoons of sweet chili sauce. The sweetness of the sauce has the added bonus of intensifying the flavor of the tomatoes.

firehouse chili con carne

makes 6 servings

PREP TIME: 10 minutes
COOK TIME: about 1 hour 45 minutes

1 tbsp vegetable oil

1 large onion, diced

2¹/₂ lbs lean ground beef

3 garlic cloves, finely chopped

¹/₄ cup chile powder

1 tbsp ground cumin

1 tsp black pepper

¹/₂ tsp chipotle chile powder

¹/₄ tsp cayenne pepper

1 tsp dried oregano

1 tsp sugar

1 large green bell pepper, seeded and diced

1 large red bell pepper, seeded and diced

1 (15 oz) can tomato sauce

2 tbsp tomato paste

2¹/₂ cups water, plus extra if needed

1 (15 oz) can pinto beans, drained but not rinsed

1 (15 oz) can kidney beans, drained but not rinsed

salt and pepper

corn muffins, to serve

To garnish

sour cream

grated cheddar cheese

fresh cilantro sprigs

Put the oil and onion into a large, heavy-based pot. Place over a medium-high heat and sauté the onion for about 5 minutes, or until beginning to soften. Add the beef and cook for about 10 minutes, breaking it up with a wooden spoon.

Add the garlic, chile powder, cumin, black pepper, chipotle chile powder, cayenne pepper, oregano and sugar. Cook, stirring, for 2 minutes.

Stir in the green pepper, red pepper, tomato sauce, tomato paste and water. Bring to a simmer, then reduce the heat to medium-low and cook, uncovered, stirring occasionally, for 1 hour.

Stir in the pinto beans and kidney beans and simmer for a further 30 minutes. Taste and season with salt and pepper. Add more water if necessary. Serve hot, garnished with the sour cream, cheese and cilantro sprigs, accompanied by corn muffins.

tip This winter warmer can be served with baked potatoes or some plain boiled rice to make a really substantial meal.

chicken noodle soup

makes 6 servings

PREP TIME: 10 minutes

COOK TIME: about 4 hours

oil, for greasing

1 large whole chicken, 4–5 lbs

salt and pepper

3 carrots, (1 chopped, 2 diced)

5 celery sticks (1 chopped, 4 diced)

2 onions (1 chopped, 1 diced)

8 cups water, plus extra if needed

1 garlic clove, peeled

4 fresh thyme sprigs

1 bay leaf

1 whole clove

1 tsp ketchup

1 tbsp butter

1/4 tsp poultry seasoning

14 oz dried egg noodles

1 tbsp chopped fresh parsley

whole-wheat bread, to serve

Preheat the oven to 450°F. Grease a 9 x 13-inch baking pan.

Season the chicken inside and out with salt and pepper. Add the chopped carrot, chopped celery and chopped onion to the prepared pan, and place the chicken on top. Roast in the preheated oven for 60 minutes, or until a thermometer inserted in the thickest part of a thigh registers 160°F.

Remove the chicken from the oven and leave to stand until cool enough to handle. Pull off the breast meat and the larger pieces of thigh and leg meat, and chill until required.

Transfer the chicken carcass and vegetables from the pan into a large pot. Add the water, garlic, thyme, bay leaf, clove and ketchup. Bring to a boil, reduce the heat to low and simmer for 2 hours. The liquid level should remain about the same, so add a splash of water to the pan from time to time.

Meanwhile, melt the butter in a large pot over a medium-low heat. Add the diced carrot, diced celery and diced onion and sauté for about 15 minutes, until they begin to soften. Stir in the poultry seasoning and remove from the heat.

Skim the fat from the top of the chicken broth, strain it into the pot with the vegetables and bring to a boil. Reduce the heat to low and simmer until the vegetables are tender. Season to taste with salt and pepper. Increase the heat to high, add the noodles and boil for 7 minutes. Dice the chicken and add to the pot. Reduce the heat to medium and simmer until the noodles are tender.

Stir in the parsley and serve immediately with the whole-wheat bread.

soups and stews

spiced pumpkin soup

makes 4 servings

PREP TIME: 15 minutes

COOK TIME: about 1 hour

2 tbsp olive oil

1 onion, chopped

1 garlic clove, chopped

1 tbsp chopped fresh ginger

1 small red chile, seeded and finely chopped

2 tbsp chopped fresh cilantro

1 bay leaf

2 lb 4 oz pumpkin, peeled, seeded, and diced

2½ cups vegetable stock

salt and pepper

half-and-half, to garnish

Heat the oil in a large saucepan over medium heat. Add the onion and garlic and cook, stirring, for about 4 minutes, until slightly softened. Add the ginger, chile, cilantro, bay leaf, and pumpkin and cook for another 3 minutes.

Pour in the stock and bring to a boil. Using a slotted spoon, skim any foam from the surface. Reduce the heat and simmer gently, stirring occasionally, for about 25 minutes, or until the pumpkin is tender. Remove from the heat, take out the bay leaf, and let cool a little.

Transfer the soup to a food processor or blender and process until smooth (you may have to do this in batches). Return the mixture to the rinsed-out pan and season to taste with salt and pepper. Reheat gently, stirring. Remove from the heat, pour into warmed soup bowls, garnish each one with a swirl of half-and-half, and serve.

variation   You can replace the pumpkin with other winter squashes—acorn and butternut squash make particularly good soups and are equally valuable sources of essential vitamin A.

chili bean stew

makes 4–6 servings

PREP TIME: 20 minutes
COOK TIME: about 45 minutes

2 tbsp olive oil

1 onion, chopped

2–4 garlic cloves, chopped

2 fresh red chiles, seeded
and sliced

1 cup drained and rinsed canned
kidney beans

1 cup drained and rinsed canned
cannellini beans

1 cup drained and rinsed canned
chickpeas

1 tbsp tomato paste

3–3^1/$_2$ cups vegetable stock

1 red bell pepper, seeded and
chopped

4 tomatoes, chopped

1 cup shelled fresh fava beans

1 tbsp chopped fresh cilantro,
plus extra to garnish

salt and pepper

paprika, to garnish

sour cream, to serve

Heat the oil in a large, heavy Dutch oven with a tight-fitting lid. Add the onion, garlic and chiles and cook, stirring frequently, for 5 minutes, until soft.

Add the kidney beans, cannellini beans and chickpeas. Blend the tomato paste with a little of the stock and pour over the bean mixture, then add the remaining stock.

Bring to a boil, then reduce the heat and simmer for 10–15 minutes. Add the red bell pepper, tomatoes and fava beans.

Simmer for an additional 15–20 minutes, or until all the vegetables are tender. Stir in most of the chopped cilantro and season to taste with salt and pepper.

Garnish with the remaining chopped cilantro and a pinch of paprika and serve topped with spoonfuls of sour cream.

old-fashioned chicken stew

makes 6 servings

PREP TIME: 15 minutes

COOK TIME: about 2 hours

2 tbsp vegetable oil

1 whole (4-5 lbs) chicken, cut into quarters

4 cups chicken broth

3 cups water

4 garlic cloves, peeled

1 bay leaf

4 sprigs fresh thyme

5 tbsp butter

2 carrots, cut into ½-inch pieces

2 celery stalks, cut into ½-inch pieces

1 large onion, chopped

5 tbsp flour

1½ tsp salt

dash of hot sauce

pepper

Dumplings

1¾ cups all-purpose flour

1 tsp salt

2 tsp baking powder

¼ tsp baking soda

3 tbsp cold butter

2 tbsp thinly sliced scallion tops

¼ cup buttermilk

¾ cup milk

Put the oil in a Dutch oven over high heat. Add the chicken pieces and brown, then add the broth, water, garlic, bay leaf and thyme. Bring to a boil, then reduce the heat to medium and simmer, covered, for 30 minutes. Uncover, transfer the chicken to a bowl, and let cool. Strain the cooking liquid into a separate bowl, skimming off any fat that rises to the top.

Add the butter, carrots, celery and onion to the Dutch oven and sauté for 5 minutes before carefully stirring in the flour. Cook for an additional 2 minutes, then whisk in the reserved cooking liquid, 1 cup at a time. Add the salt, hot sauce, and pepper to taste. Reduce the heat to low and simmer, covered, for 30 minutes, until the vegetables are tender.

Remove the chicken meat from the bones and tear into chunks. Stir the chicken pieces into the cooked vegetables. Cover and reduce the heat to low.

To make the dumplings, put the flour, salt, baking powder and baking soda into a mixing bowl and stir. Add the butter and cut in until the mixture resembles coarse breadcrumbs. Add the scallion tops, buttermilk and milk and stir with a fork until a thick dough forms.

Stir the stew and drop large balls of the dumpling dough into the mixture. Cover and cook for 15 minutes over medium heat. The dumplings are done when they are firm and cooked in the center. Turn off the heat and serve in warmed bowls.

hearty beef stew

makes 4 servings

PREP TIME: 20 minutes

COOK TIME: about 2 hours
30 minutes

3 lbs boneless chuck roast,
cut into 2-inch pieces

salt and pepper

2 tbsp vegetable oil

2 yellow onions, cut into 1-inch
pieces

3 tbsp flour

3 garlic cloves, finely chopped

4 cups cold beef stock or broth

3 carrots, peeled and cut into
1-inch pieces

2 celery stalks, cut into 1-inch
pieces

1 tbsp ketchup

1 bay leaf

¼ tsp dried rosemary

¼ tsp dried thyme

1 tsp salt

2 lbs Yukon gold potatoes,
peeled and cut into large chunks

salt and pepper

fresh flat-leaf parsley, to garnish
(optional)

Season the beef very generously with salt and pepper. Add the oil to a large, heavy-bottom pot or Dutch oven with a tight-fitting lid, and set over high heat. When the oil begins to smoke slightly, add the beef and brown very well. Work in batches if necessary. Once it is well-browned, transfer the beef to a bowl using a slotted spoon, leaving the oil and beef drippings in the pan.

Reduce the heat to medium, add the onions to the pan, and sauté for about 5 minutes, or until translucent. Add the flour and cook for 2 minutes, stirring frequently. Add the garlic and cook for 1 minute. Whisk in 1 cup of the stock to deglaze the bottom of the pan, scraping up any browned bits that are stuck to the bottom.

Add the remaining broth, carrots, celery, ketchup, bay leaf, rosemary, thyme, beef and salt. Bring back to a gentle simmer, cover, and cook over low heat for 1 hour. Add the potatoes and simmer, covered, for an additional 30 minutes. Remove the cover, increase the heat to medium, and cook, stirring occasionally, for an additional 30 minutes, or until the meat and vegetables are tender. (This final 30 minutes of cooking will reduce and thicken the sauce. If the stew gets too thick, add some more stock or water.)

Turn off the heat, taste, and adjust the seasoning, then let sit for 15 minutes before serving. Garnish with parsley, if using.

beef casserole with dumplings

makes 6 servings

PREP TIME: 20 minutes
COOK TIME: 3 hours

3 tbsp olive oil

2 onions, finely sliced

2 garlic cloves, chopped

2 lbs boneless beef chuck or beef round, trimmed and cut into strips

2 tbsp all-purpose flour

salt and pepper

1 cup beef stock

boquet garni (1 sprig each parsley and thyme and 1 bay leaf tied together with kitchen twine)

²/₃ cup red wine

salt and pepper

Herb dumplings

1 cup self-rising flour

¹/₂ cup vegetable shortening or lard

1 tsp mustard

1 tbsp chopped fresh parsley, plus extra to garnish

1 tsp chopped fresh sage

salt and pepper

¹/₄ cup cold water

Preheat the oven to 300°F.

Heat 1 tbsp of the oil in a large, enameled cast-iron dish with a tight-fitting lid or Dutch oven and sauté the onions and garlic until soft and brown. Transfer to a plate.

Heat the remaining oil in the dish. Add the beef, in batches, and cook, stirring frequently, for 8–10 minutes, until browned all over.

Sprinkle in the flour and stir well. Season well with salt and pepper. Pour in the stock, stirring all the time, then bring to a boil. Return the onions to the dish with the bouquet garni and wine. Cover and bake in the preheated oven for 2–2¹/₂ hours.

For the dumplings, place the flour, shortening, mustard, parsley and sage in a bowl and season with salt and pepper. Mix well, then add enough of the water to form a slightly soft dough. Break the dough into 12 pieces and roll them into round dumplings.

Remove the dish from the oven, discard the bouquet garni, and add the dumplings, pushing them down under the liquid. Cover, return to the oven, and bake for an additional 15 minutes, until the dumplings have doubled in size. Garnish with parsley and serve immediately.

slow and delicious
slow-cooker
favorites

italian slow-braised beef

makes 6 servings

PREP TIME: 10 minutes, plus
12 hours marinating time

COOK TIME: about 8 hours

1¼ cups red wine

¼ cup olive oil

1 celery stalk, chopped

2 shallots, sliced

4 garlic cloves, finely chopped

1 bay leaf

10 fresh basil leaves, plus extra
to garnish

3 fresh parsley sprigs

pinch of grated nutmeg

pinch of ground cinnamon

2 cloves

3¼ lbs bottom round roast or
rump roast

1-2 garlic cloves, thinly sliced

2 oz bacon or pancetta,
chopped

1 (14.5-oz) can diced tomatoes

2 tbsp tomato paste

Combine the wine, half of the oil, celery, shallots, garlic, herbs and spices in a large nonmetallic bowl. Add the beef, cover, and let marinate, turning occasionally, for 12 hours.

Drain the beef, reserving the marinade, and pat dry with paper towels. Make small incisions all over the beef using a sharp knife. Insert a slice of garlic and a piece of bacon in each "pocket." Heat the remaining oil in a large skillet. Add the meat and cook over medium heat, turning frequently, until evenly browned. Transfer to a slow cooker.

Strain the reserved marinade into the skillet and bring to a boil. Stir in the tomatoes and tomato paste. Stir well, then pour the mixture over the beef. Cover and cook on low for about 8–9 hours, until the beef is cooked to your liking. If possible, turn the beef over halfway through the cooking time.

Remove the beef from the slow cooker and place on a cutting board. Cover with aluminum foil and let rest for 10–15 minutes until firm. Cut into slices and transfer to a serving plate. Spoon over the sauce, garnish with basil leaves, and serve immediately.

chicken cacciatore

makes 4 servings

PREP TIME: 10 minutes
COOK TIME: about 5 hours and 30 minutes

3 tbsp olive oil

4 skinless chicken pieces

2 onions, sliced

2 garlic cloves, finely chopped

1 (14.5-oz) can diced tomatoes

1 tbsp tomato paste

2 tbsp chopped fresh parsley

2 tsp fresh thyme leaves, plus extra sprigs to garnish

$^2/_3$ cup red wine

salt and pepper

Heat the oil in a heavy skillet. Add the chicken and cook over medium heat, turning occasionally, for 10 minutes, until golden all over. Using a slotted spoon, transfer the chicken to a slow cooker.

Add the onions to the skillet and cook, stirring occasionally, for 5 minutes, until softened and just turning golden. Add the garlic, tomatoes, tomato paste, parsley, thyme leaves and wine. Season with salt and pepper and bring to a boil.

Pour the tomato mixture over the chicken parts. Cover and cook on low for 5 hours, until the chicken is tender and cooked through. Taste and adjust the seasoning, adding salt and pepper if needed. Transfer to warm serving plates, garnish with thyme sprigs, and serve immediately.

fact This hearty dish is traditionally served to Italian hunters at the end of a long day out in the open air. The chicken benefits from the long, slow cooking, resulting in a versatile dish that can be served with potatoes, pasta, rice or polenta.

lamb with spring vegetables

makes 4–6 servings

PREP TIME: 15 minutes
COOK TIME: about 9 hours

⅓ cup olive oil

6 shallots, chopped

1 garlic clove, chopped

2 celery stalks, chopped

1 tbsp all-purpose flour

salt and pepper

1½ lbs boned leg or shoulder of lamb, cut into 1-inch cubes

3½ cups chicken stock

1½ cup pearled barley, rinsed

4 small turnips, halved

15 baby carrots

1½ cups frozen young green peas, thawed

1½ cups frozen baby fava beans, thawed

chopped fresh parsley, to garnish

Heat 3 tbsp of the oil in a large pot. Add the shallots, garlic and celery and cook over low heat, stirring occasionally, for 8–10 minutes, until softened and lightly browned.

Meanwhile, put the flour into a plastic resealable bag and season well with salt and pepper. Add the lamb cubes, in batches, seal the top securely, and shake well to coat. Transfer the meat to a plate.

Using a slotted spoon, transfer the softened vegetables to a slow cooker. Add the remaining oil to the pot and heat. Add the lamb, in batches if necessary, increase the heat to medium, and cook, stirring frequently, for 8–10 minutes, until evenly browned.

Return all the lamb to the pan. Gradually stir in the stock, scraping up the browned bits from the bottom of the pan. Stir in the pearled barley, turnips and carrots, season to taste with salt and pepper, and bring to a boil. Transfer the mixture to the slow cooker and stir well. Cover and cook on low for 8–10 hours, until the lamb is tender.

Add the green peas and fava beans to the slow cooker, sprinkling them evenly on top of the stew. Re-cover and cook on low for an additional 30 minutes, until heated through. Stir well, then taste and adjust the seasoning, adding salt and pepper if needed. Garnish with parsley and serve immediately.

pork with peppers and apricots

makes 4 servings

PREP TIME: 10 minutes

COOK TIME: about 9 hours

2 tbsp olive oil

4 pork chops, trimmed of excess fat

1 shallot, chopped

2 garlic cloves, finely chopped

2 orange bell peppers, seeded and sliced

1 tbsp all-purpose flour

2½ cups chicken stock

1 tbsp medium-hot Indian curry paste

1 cup dried apricots

salt and pepper

baby spinach leaves and cooked couscous, to serve

Heat the oil in a large skillet. Add the chops and cook over medium heat for 2–4 minutes on each side, until evenly browned. Remove with tongs and put them into a slow cooker.

Add the shallot, garlic and bell peppers to the skillet, reduce the heat, and cook, stirring occasionally, for 5 minutes, until softened. Stir in the flour and cook, stirring continuously, for 1 minute.

Gradually stir in the stock, a little at a time, then add the curry paste and apricots. Bring to a boil, stirring occasionally.

Season to taste with salt and pepper and transfer the mixture to the slow cooker. Cover and cook on low for 8–9 hours, until the meat is tender.

Transfer to warm serving plates and serve immediately with baby spinach and couscous.

variation Replace the pork with 4 skinned chicken breasts and cook in exactly the same way for an equally delicious dish.

easy chinese chicken

makes 4 servings

PREP TIME: 10 minutes
COOK TIME: about 4 hours

2 tsp grated fresh ginger

4 garlic cloves, finely chopped

2 star anise or 1 tsp five-spice powder

²/₃ cup Chinese rice wine or medium-dry sherry

2 tbsp dark soy sauce

1 tsp sesame oil

¹/₃ cup water

4 skinless chicken thighs or drumsticks

shredded scallions, to garnish

cooked rice, to serve

Mix together the ginger, garlic, star anise, rice wine, soy sauce, sesame oil and water in a wide, shallow pot, add the chicken and bring to a boil.

Transfer to the slow cooker, cover, and cook on low for 4 hours, or until the chicken is tender and cooked through.

Remove and discard the star anise. Transfer the chicken to warm serving plates, garnish with shredded scallions, and serve immediately with rice.

variation For a different finish and flavor, replace the scallion garnish with a handful of roughly chopped fresh cilantro.

turkey-and-rice casserole

makes 4 servings

PREP TIME: 10 minutes
COOK TIME: about 2 hours

1 tbsp olive oil

1 lb boneless, skinless turkey breast, diced

1 onion, diced

2 carrots, diced

2 celery stalks, sliced

3½ cups sliced white button mushrooms

1 cup long-grain rice

salt and pepper

2 cups hot chicken stock

Heat the oil in a heavy skillet, add the turkey, and cook over high heat for 3–4 minutes, until lightly browned.

Combine the onion, carrots, celery, mushrooms and rice in the slow cooker. Arrange the turkey on top, season well with salt and pepper, and pour the stock over. Cover and cook on high for 2 hours.

Stir lightly with a fork to mix, adjust the seasoning to taste and serve immediately.

variation To give a greater depth of flavor to the casserole, add ¼ cup chopped dried porcini mushrooms to the slow cooker with the other vegetables. There's no need to presoak them—the slow cooking will do that for you.

baked eggplant and zucchini

makes 4 servings

PREP TIME: 10 minutes
COOK TIME: 4 hours 15 minutes

2 large eggplants
olive oil, for brushing
2 large zucchini, sliced
4 tomatoes, sliced
1 garlic clove, finely chopped
salt and pepper
⅓ cup dry breadcrumbs
3 tbsp grated Parmesan cheese
basil leaves, to garnish

Cut the eggplants into fairly thin slices and brush with oil. Heat a large, ridged grill pan or heavy skillet over high heat, then add the eggplants and cook in batches for 6–8 minutes, turning once, until soft and brown.

Layer the eggplants in the slow cooker with the zucchini, tomatoes and garlic, seasoning with salt and pepper between the layers.

Mix the breadcrumbs with the cheese and sprinkle over the vegetables. Cover and cook on low for 4 hours.

Transfer to warm serving bowls, garnish with basil leaves, and serve immediately.

fact Although eggplant is always used as a vegetable, it is actually a fruit, related to the tomato. Grown in many different shapes and sizes, and in various colors from white to deepest purple, it is widely used in Middle Eastern and Mediterranean countries, where it is a versatile ingredient in a wide variety of dishes. In Italy it is often referred to as "poor man's meat."

moroccan lamb stew

makes 6 servings

PREP TIME: 15 minutes

COOK TIME: 8 hours 45 minutes

3 tbsp olive oil

2 red onions, chopped

2 garlic cloves, finely chopped

1-inch piece fresh ginger, finely chopped

1 yellow bell pepper, seeded and chopped

2 1/4 lbs boneless lamb shoulder, trimmed and cut into 1-inch cubes

3 1/2 cups lamb stock or chicken stock

1 3/4 cups dried apricots, halved

1 tbsp honey

1/4 cup lemon juice

pinch of saffron threads

2-inch cinnamon stick

salt and pepper

toasted slivered almonds and fresh cilantro sprigs, to garnish

Heat the oil in a large, heavy Dutch oven. Add the onions, garlic, ginger and yellow bell pepper and cook over low heat, stirring occasionally, for 5 minutes, until the onion has softened. Add the lamb and stir well to mix, then pour in the stock. Add the apricots, honey, lemon juice, saffron and cinnamon stick and season to taste with salt and pepper. Bring to a boil.

Transfer the mixture to the slow cooker. Cover and cook on low for 8 1/2 hours, until the meat is tender.

Remove and discard the cinnamon stick. Transfer to warm serving bowls and garnish with slivered almonds and cilantro sprigs. Serve immediately.

fact Traditionally cooked in a tagine, the North African earthenware predecessor of the electric crockpot, this meltingly delicious stew is a slow-cooking classic.

spring vegetable risotto

makes 4 servings

PREP TIME: 15 minutes
COOK TIME: about 3 hours
15 minutes

5 cups vegetable stock
large pinch of saffron threads
4 tbsp salted butter
1 tbsp olive oil
1 onion, chopped
2 garlic cloves, finely chopped
1¼ cups arborio rice
3 tbsp dry white wine
salt and pepper
1 bay leaf
9 oz young mixed vegetables,
such as asparagus spears, green
beans, baby carrots, baby fava
beans and young green peas,
thawed if frozen
2 tbsp chopped flat-leaf parsley
²/₃ cup grated Parmesan cheese

Put ¹/₃ cup of the stock into a small bowl, crumble in the saffron threads, and let steep. Reserve ²/₃ cup of the remaining stock and heat the remainder in a saucepan.

Meanwhile, melt half of the butter with the oil in a separate large saucepan. Add the onion and garlic and cook over low heat, stirring occasionally, for 5 minutes, until softened. Stir in the rice and cook, stirring thoroughly, for 1–2 minutes, until all the grains are coated and glistening. Pour in the wine and cook, stirring thoroughly, for a few minutes, until all the alcohol has evaporated. Season to taste with salt and pepper. Pour in the hot stock and the saffron mixture, add the bay leaf, and bring to a boil, stirring thoroughly.

Transfer the mixture to the slow cooker, cover, and cook on low for 2 hours. Meanwhile, if using fresh vegetables, slice the asparagus spears, green beans and carrots and blanch all the vegetables in boiling water for 5 minutes. Drain and reserve.

Stir the reserved stock into the rice mixture if it seems dry, and add the mixed vegetables, sprinkling them evenly over the top. Re-cover and cook on low for an additional 30–45 minutes, until heated through.

Remove and discard the bay leaf. Gently stir in the parsley, the remaining butter and the cheese and serve immediately.

meals *in* minutes

pork in plum sauce

makes 4 servings

PREP TIME: 15 minutes
COOK TIME: 30 minutes

9 oz medium egg noodles

1 lb 5 oz pork tenderloin

2 tbsp peanut oil

1 orange bell pepper, seeded and sliced

1 bunch of scallions, sliced

3²/₃ cups sliced oyster mushrooms

5¹/₄ cups fresh bean sprouts

2 tbsp dry sherry

²/₃ cup plum sauce

salt and pepper

chopped fresh cilantro, to garnish

Bring a large saucepan of heavily salted water to a boil. Once boiling, add the noodles and cook according to package instructions. Drain, rinse in cold water and set aside.

Slice the pork into long, thin strips.

Heat the oil in a wok and stir-fry the pork for 2–3 minutes.

Add the bell pepper and stir-fry for 2 minutes, then add the scallions, mushrooms and bean sprouts. Stir-fry for 2–3 minutes, then add the sherry and plum sauce and heat until boiling.

Add the noodles and toss until coated in sauce and heated through. Season with salt and pepper. Garnish with cilantro and serve.

turkey cutlets with prosciutto and sage

makes 2 servings

PREP TIME: 15 minutes

COOK TIME: about 2 minutes

2 boneless, skinless turkey cutlets

salt and pepper

2 slices prosciutto, halved

4 fresh sage leaves

2 tbsp all-purpose flour

2 tbsp olive oil

1 tbsp butter

lemon wedges, to serve

Slice each turkey cutlet in half horizontally into 2 thinner scallops.

Put each scallop between 2 sheets of plastic wrap and pound out thinly with a rolling pin. Season each scallop with salt and pepper to taste.

Lay a half slice of prosciutto on each scallop, put a sage leaf on top, and secure with a toothpick.

Mix the flour with salt and pepper to taste on a large plate. Dust both sides of each scallop with the seasoned flour.

Heat the oil in a large skillet, add the butter, and heat until foaming. Add the scallops and fry over high heat for 1½ minutes, sage-side down.

Turn the scallops over and fry for an additional 30 seconds, until golden brown and cooked through. Remove toothpick and serve immediately with lemon wedges.

tip This delicious, light variation of traditional saltimbocca would be an extra-special treat with the addition of a little Marsala. Remove the cooked cutlets from the skillet and keep warm, then add 1 tablespoon of Marsala to the skillet and bring to a boil. Pour over the turkey and serve immediately.

meals in minutes

hot-smoked salmon
on hash browns

makes 4 servings

PREP TIME: 10 minutes

COOK TIME: about 30 minutes

1 onion, peeled

1 lb 2 oz Russet potatoes, peeled

2 tbsp chopped fresh dill, plus
extra sprigs to garnish

1 tsp celery salt

pepper

2 tbsp butter

2 tbsp olive oil

1 bunch watercress

1 tbsp walnut oil

2 tbsp lemon juice

9 oz hot-smoked salmon,
coarsely flaked

pepper

lemon wedges, to serve

Grate the onion and potatoes in a food processor. Transfer to a
clean dish towel and squeeze out as much moisture as possible.

Stir in the chopped dill and celery salt and season well with pepper.
Divide into 8 portions.

Melt half the butter and half the olive oil in a large nonstick skillet.
Add 4 heaps of the potato mixture and flatten lightly. Fry for 4–5
minutes, until golden underneath.

Flip the hash browns over to cook on the other side until golden
brown. Remove from the skillet and keep warm while you repeat
this step with the remaining mixture.

Toss the watercress with the walnut oil and 1 tbsp of the lemon
juice. Divide among serving plates and place the hash browns
on top.

Top with the salmon and sprinkle with the remaining lemon juice
and pepper to taste.

Garnish with dill sprigs and serve with lemon wedges.

steamed chicken with chile-and-cilantro butter

makes 4 servings

PREP TIME: 5 minutes, plus time for butter to soften
COOK TIME: about 40 minutes

4 tbsp butter, softened
1 fresh Thai chile, seeded and chopped
3 tbsp chopped fresh cilantro
4 boneless, skinless
chicken breasts, about 6 oz each
salt and pepper

1 3/4 cups coconut milk
1 1/2 cups chicken stock
1 cup basmati rice

Pickled vegetables
1 carrot
1/2 cucumber
3 scallions
2 tbsp rice vinegar

Mix the butter with the chile and cilantro.

Cut a deep slash into the side of each chicken breast to form a pocket.

Spoon a quarter of the flavored butter into each pocket and place on a 12-inch square of parchment paper.

Season to taste with salt and pepper, then bring together 2 opposite sides of the paper on top, folding over to seal firmly. Twist the ends to seal.

Pour the coconut milk and stock into a large pan with a steamer top. Bring to a boil. Stir in the rice with a pinch of salt.

Put the chicken parcels in the steamer top, cover, and simmer for 15–18 minutes, stirring the rice once, until the rice is tender and the chicken is cooked through.

Meanwhile, trim the carrot, cucumber and scallions and cut into fine sticks. Sprinkle with the vinegar.

Unwrap the chicken, reserving the juices, and cut in half diagonally.

Serve the chicken on the rice, with the juices spooned over and pickled vegetables on the side.

meals in minutes

seared sesame salmon
with bok choy

makes 4 servings

PREP TIME: about 5 minutes
COOK TIME: 20 minutes

1-inch piece fresh ginger
1 tbsp soy sauce
1 tsp sesame oil
4 skinless salmon fillets
2 tbsp sesame seeds
2 small bok choy
1 bunch of scallions
1 tbsp vegetable oil
1 tsp sesame oil
salt and pepper
lime wedges, to serve

Peel and finely grate the ginger, then combine with the soy sauce and sesame oil in a shallow dish that is large enough to hold the salmon fillets in a single layer.

Add the salmon fillets, turning to coat evenly on both sides.

Sprinkle one side of the salmon with half the sesame seeds, then turn and sprinkle the other side with the remaining sesame seeds.

Cut the bok choy lengthwise into quarters. Cut the scallions into thick diagonal slices.

Preheat a heavy-bottom nonstick skillet over high heat. Add the salmon and cook for 3–4 minutes. Turn and cook for an additional 3–4 minutes.

Meanwhile, heat the vegetable and sesame oils in a wok. Add the bok choy and scallions, and stir-fry for 2–3 minutes. Season to taste with salt and pepper.

Divide the vegetables among warmed serving plates and put the salmon on top.

Serve immediately with lime wedges for squeezing over.

hot sesame beef

makes 4 servings

PREP TIME: about 25 minutes
COOK TIME: about 20 minutes

1 lb 2 oz beef tenderloin, cut into thin strips

1 tbsp sesame seeds

½ cup beef stock

2 tbsp soy sauce

2 tbsp grated fresh ginger

2 garlic cloves, finely chopped

1 tsp cornstarch

1 tsp chile flakes

3 tbsp sesame oil

1 large head broccoli, cut into florets

1 yellow bell pepper, seeded and thinly sliced

1 fresh red chile, finely sliced

1 tbsp chili oil, to taste

salt and pepper

cooked wild rice, to serve

1 tbsp chopped fresh cilantro, to garnish

Mix the beef strips with the sesame seeds in a small bowl.

In a separate bowl, stir together the stock, soy sauce, ginger, garlic, cornstarch and chile flakes.

Heat 1 tbsp of the sesame oil in a wok. Stir-fry the beef for 2–3 minutes. Remove and set aside, then wipe the wok clean with paper towels.

Heat the remaining sesame oil in the wok, add the broccoli, bell pepper, chile and chili oil and stir-fry for 2–3 minutes.

Stir in the stock mixture, cover, and simmer for 2 minutes.

Return the beef to the wok and simmer until the juices thicken, stirring occasionally. Cook for an additional 1–2 minutes. Season to taste with salt and pepper.

Serve over wild rice and garnish with cilantro.

I love to grill on Sundays. The nice part about marinated skirt steak is you can prep the marinade watching a game and sear the steak during a long commercial break!

marinated skirt steak

serves 3–4

■ ■ ■

Jen and Bill Klein
The Little Couple

PREP TIME: 40 minutes
COOK TIME: 5 minutes

1½ to 2 lbs of trimmed skirt steak (I am a lean meat guy—you get what you like) and cut into 3 or 4 equal-size pieces

1 cup olive oil

2–3 scallions, wash and cut scallions into what I call ½-inch long O's

½ cup Kikkoman soy sauce

1–2 tbsp Worcestershire sauce, depending on affinity for Worcestershire flavor

¼ cup Coca-Cola

2–3 cloves garlic, minced or sliced small

1 tsp crushed red pepper flakes,

2 tsp brown sugar

Add all ingredients except for the steak, to a large zip-close bag (one you can trust not to leak!). Shake around a bit to mix things up. Open the bag and place or drop in your 3-4 pieces of steak. Allow the steak to marinate for 20-30 minutes. You should preheat your grill to searing heat (450° or higher). If you have a searing burner on your grill. . . now is the time to use that bad boy.

Place the skirt-steak pieces on the grill for just minutes. Skirt steaks are thin and can be overcooked and get rubbery very quickly... so be careful not to get too caught up in the game. Flip the steaks over and cook again (3 minutes per side for medium rare, a little longer for the non-mooing fans).

Let the steak stand for about 5 minutes before slicing. Slicing the steak is a key part of this meal. You MUST cut against the grain with the skirt steak. Half-inch to 1-inch slices work perfectly.

Grab your fork and your beer. If you feel compelled, grab some washed arugula salad with balsamic vinegar and oil, a few cherry tomatoes and a sprinkle of pepper as bedding for your awesome skirt steak.

egg tortilla with feta and corn

makes 2 servings

PREP TIME: 10 minutes
COOK TIME: about 20 minutes

12 oz potatoes
2 tbsp olive oil
1 onion, chopped
1 zucchini, coarsely grated
7 oz canned corn, drained
6 large eggs
salt and pepper
1 cup crumbled feta cheese
paprika, to garnish

Preheat the broiler to high. Peel or scrub the potatoes and cut into $\frac{1}{2}$-inch dice.

Cook the potatoes in a saucepan of lightly salted boiling water for 5 minutes, or until just tender. Drain.

Heat the oil in a large ovenproof skillet over medium heat and fry the onion for about 5 minutes, until softened.

Stir in the zucchini and potatoes, cook for 2 minutes, then stir in the corn.

Beat the eggs lightly with salt and pepper to taste.

Stir the beaten eggs into the skillet, then scatter over the feta cheese. Cook for 4–6 minutes, until almost set.

Put the tortilla under the preheated broiler for 2–3 minutes, until set and golden-brown.

Sprinkle with paprika and cut into 4–6 wedges.

Serve hot or cold.

tip   Bring some bright color and flavor to this dish by adding half a diced red bell pepper with the zucchini.

baked tapenade chicken

makes 4 servings

PREP TIME: 5 minutes
COOK TIME: 35 minutes

4 boneless, skinless chicken
breasts
¼ cup green-olive tapenade
8 thin slices pancetta
2 garlic cloves, coarsely
chopped
9 oz cherry tomatoes, halved
salt and pepper
½ cup dry white wine
2 tbsp olive oil
8 slices ciabatta

Preheat the oven to 425°F. Put the chicken breasts on a cutting board
and cut three deep slashes into each.

Spread 1 tbsp of the tapenade over each chicken breast, pushing it into
the slashes. Wrap each chicken breast in two slices of pancetta. Place the
chicken breasts in a shallow ovenproof dish and arrange the garlic and
tomatoes around them. Season to taste with salt and pepper, then pour
over the wine and 1 tbsp of the oil.

Bake in the preheated oven for about 20 minutes, until the juices run
clear when the chicken is pierced with a skewer.

Remove from oven, cover loosely with aluminum foil and let stand for
5 minutes.

Meanwhile, preheat the broiler to high. Brush the ciabatta with the
remaining oil and cook under the preheated broiler for 2–3 minutes,
turning once, until golden.

Transfer the chicken and tomatoes to serving plates and spoon over the
juices. Serve with the toasted ciabatta.

meals in minutes

grilled turkey cutlets
with lemon

makes 4 servings

PREP TIME: about 10 minutes,
plus 30 minutes marinating time
COOK TIME: 10 minutes

1 lemon

2 tbsp olive oil

1 garlic clove, crushed

4 turkey cutlets

salt and pepper

salad, to serve

Finely grate the zest from the lemon and squeeze the juice. Mix together the lemon juice and zest, oil, and garlic in a wide, nonmetallic dish.

Place the turkey cutlets in the lemon mixture, turning to coat evenly. Cover with plastic wrap and chill in the refrigerator for 30 minutes. Drain the turkey, discarding the marinade, and season with salt and pepper.

Heat a ridged grill pan over high heat. Place the turkey cutlets in the pan, and cook for about 4 minutes per side or until golden.

To check that the meat is cooked through, cut into the middle to check that there are no remaining traces of pink or red. Any juices that run out should be clear and piping hot with visible steam rising.

Transfer the turkey to a warm plate, cover with aluminum foil, and let stand for 3–4 minutes before serving.

Serve with salad.

quick and creamy fish pie

makes 4 servings

PREP TIME: 15 minutes
COOK TIME: 25 minutes

1 tbsp olive oil

2 shallots, finely chopped

²/₃ cup dry white wine

1 bay leaf

2 ³/₄ cups thickly sliced mushrooms

¹/₂ cup sour cream

1 lb 2 oz firm whitefish fillets, cut into chunks

salt and pepper

6 oz cooked, peeled shrimp

1¹/₂ cups frozen peas

3 tbsp melted butter

2 ³/₄ cups fresh white breadcrumbs

chopped fresh parsley, to garnish

Preheat the broiler to medium. Heat the oil in a large ovenproof skillet or a shallow Dutch oven and fry the shallots for 2–3 minutes, until softened.

Add the wine, bay leaf and mushrooms and simmer for 2 minutes, stirring occasionally.

Stir in the sour cream and add the fish. Season to taste with salt and pepper.

Bring to a boil, cover, and simmer for 5–6 minutes, until the fish is almost cooked.

Remove the bay leaf, add the shrimp and peas, and return to a boil.

Combine the melted butter and breadcrumbs and spread evenly over the top of the fish mixture.

Put the skillet under the preheated broiler for 3–4 minutes, until the topping is golden-brown and bubbling.

Sprinkle with parsley and serve hot.

grilled steak with hot chile salsa

makes 4 servings

PREP TIME: 10 minutes
COOK TIME: about 20 minutes

Hot chile salsa
4 fresh red habanero chiles
4 fresh green poblano chiles
3 tomatoes, peeled, seeded and diced
2 tbsp chopped fresh cilantro
1 tbsp red-wine vinegar
2 tbsp olive oil
salt

vegetable oil, for brushing
4 sirloin steaks, about 8 oz each
salt and pepper

corn salad or arugula, to garnish

Preheat the broiler to high. Arrange the chiles on a foil-lined broiler rack and cook under the preheated broiler, turning frequently, until blackened and charred.

Let cool. When cool enough to handle, peel off the skins. Halve and seed the chiles, then finely chop the flesh.

Mix together the chiles, tomatoes and cilantro in a bowl.

Add the vinegar and olive oil, season to taste with salt, toss well, cover, and chill until needed.

Heat a ridged grill pan over medium heat and brush lightly with vegetable oil. Season the steaks to taste with salt and pepper, and cook for 2–4 minutes on each side, or until cooked to your liking.

Serve immediately with the salsa and corn salad.

family
favorites

June Shannon
Here Comes Honey Boo Boo

bbq chicken and rice

makes 4–6 servings

■ ■ ■

PREP TIME: 2 minutes
COOK TIME: 25 minutes

4 tablespoons butter
6 boneless chicken breasts
3 bags of boil-in-the-bag rice
3 cups BBQ sauce

Rub 2 tbsp butter into the chicken breasts.

Heat a frying pan and add the chicken breasts. Reduce the heat and cook for 15 to 20 minutes until the chicken is cooked. The chicken is cooked when it is no longer pink in the middle. Remove from the heat

Boil the rice in the bag following the instructions on the packages.

Cut the chicken into 1-inch chunks and put in a large bowl. Add the cooked rice into the bowl and stir in the additional 2 tbsp butter.

Pour the barbecue sauce over the chicken and rice and stir together. Serve immediately.

Quick, simple and the more butter the better. MMMM Sugar Bear's favorite. . . I made this on our Thanksgiving Day.

easy roasted chicken

makes 6 servings

PREP TIME: 10 minutes
COOK TIME: 2 hours 15 minutes

1 whole chicken (5 lbs)

4 tbsp salted butter, softened

2 tbsp chopped fresh lemon thyme, plus extra sprigs to garnish

salt and pepper

1 lemon, cut into quarters

¼ cup white wine, plus extra if needed

Preheat the oven to 425°F. Place the chicken in a roasting pan.

Put the butter in a bowl, add the thyme, season with salt and pepper, and mix together, then rub the butter all over the chicken. Place the lemon inside the cavity. Pour the wine over the chicken and roast in the preheated oven for 15 minutes.

Reduce the temperature to 375°F and roast, basting frequently, for an additional 1 hour 45 minutes.

To check if the chicken is cooked through, pierce the thickest part of the leg between the drumstick and the thigh with the tip of a sharp knife or metal skewer. Any juices should be piping hot and clear with no traces of red or pink. To further check, gently pull the leg away from the body, the leg should "give" and no traces of pinkness or blood should remain. Transfer to a warmed platter, cover with foil and allow to rest for 10 minutes.

Place the roasting pan on the stove and simmer the pan juices gently over low heat until they have reduced and are thick and glossy. Season with salt and pepper and reserve.

To carve the chicken, place on a clean cutting board. Using a carving knife and fork, cut between the wings and the side of the breast. Remove the wings and cut slices off the breast. Cut the legs from the body and cut through the joint to separate the drumstick and thigh pieces.

Serve with the pan juices, garnished with thyme sprigs.

family favorites

homemade hamburgers

makes 6 servings

PREP TIME: 10 minutes, plus 30 minutes chilling time
COOK TIME: 20–30 minutes

2 lb 4 oz ground beef
1 small onion, grated
1 tbsp chopped fresh parsley
2 tsp Worcestershire sauce
salt and pepper
2 tbsp vegetable oil

6 hamburger buns, split and toasted
salad greens
tomato slices
dill pickles, sliced
ketchup

Put the ground beef, onion, parsley and Worcestershire sauce into a bowl, season with salt and pepper to taste, and mix well with your hands until thoroughly combined.

Divide the mixture into 6 equal portions and gently form into patties. If you have time, chill in the refrigerator for 30 minutes to firm up.

Heat the oil in a large skillet. Add the hamburgers, in batches, and cook over medium heat for 5–8 minutes on each side, turning them carefully with a spatula. Remove from the skillet and keep warm while you cook the remaining hamburgers.

Serve in toasted hamburger buns with salad greens, tomato slices, dill pickles and ketchup.

tip Fresh thyme is the beef flavor enhancer—add 1 tablespoon of the chopped fresh herb with the parsley to give your burgers that extra wow! factor.

pot roast

makes 6 servings

PREP TIME: 15 minutes

COOK TIME: 3 hours 30 minutes

4–5 Yukon gold potatoes, cut into large chunks

2¹/₂ tbsp all-purpose flour

salt and pepper

3¹/₂ lbs beef chuck roast

2 tbsp vegetable oil

2 tbsp butter

1 onion, finely chopped

2 celery stalks, diced

2 carrots, diced

1 tsp dill seed

1 tsp dried thyme

1¹/₂ cups red wine

¹/₃–¹/₂ cup beef stock

2 tbsp chopped fresh dill, to serve

Bring a large saucepan of lightly salted water to a boil. Add the potatoes, bring back to a boil, and cook for 10 minutes. Drain and set aside.

Preheat the oven to 275°F. Mix 2 tbsp of the flour with 1 tsp salt and ¹/₄ tsp pepper in a large shallow dish. Dip the meat in the flour to coat.

Heat the oil in a Dutch oven, add the meat, and brown. Transfer to a plate. Add 1 tbsp of butter to the pot, then add the onion, celery, carrots, dill seed and thyme and cook for 5 minutes.

Return the meat and juices to the pot. Pour in the wine and enough stock to reach one-third of the way up the meat and bring to a boil.

Cover and cook in the oven for 3 hours, turning the meat every 30 minutes. Add the potatoes and more stock, if necessary, after 2 hours.

When ready, transfer the meat and vegetables to a warm serving dish. Strain the cooking liquid to remove any solids, then return the liquid to the pot.

Mix the remaining butter and flour to a paste.

Bring the cooking liquid to a boil. Beat in small pieces of the flour and butter paste, beating continuously until the sauce is smooth.

Pour the sauce over the meat and vegetables. Sprinkle with fresh dill and serve.

meatballs

makes 4 servings

PREP TIME: 10 minutes
COOK TIME: 1 hour

Sauce

1 onion, cut into wedges

3 red bell peppers, halved and seeded

1 (14.5-oz) can diced tomatoes

salt and pepper

1 bay leaf

Meatballs

1 tbsp olive oil

1 small onion, finely chopped

2 garlic cloves, finely chopped

2 fresh thyme sprigs, finely chopped

1$^1\!/_2$ lbs ground beef

$^1\!/_2$ cup fresh breadcrumbs

1 large egg, lightly beaten

salt and pepper

To make the sauce, preheat the broiler. Place the onion wedges and red bell pepper halves on a foil-lined baking sheet and roast under the broiler, turning frequently, for 10 minutes, until the pepper skins are blistered and charred.

Put the peppers into a plastic bag, seal and let cool. Set the onion wedges aside. Peel off the pepper skins and coarsely chop. Put the bell peppers into a food processor with the onion and tomatoes. Process to a smooth purée and season with salt and pepper.

Pour into a saucepan with the bay leaf and bring to a boil. Reduce the heat and simmer, stirring occasionally, for 10 minutes. Keep warm while you make the meatballs.

For the meatballs, heat the oil in a skillet. Add the onion and garlic and cook over a low heat for 5 minutes, or until soft. Place in a bowl with the thyme, ground beef, breadcrumbs and egg. Season to taste with salt and pepper, mix thoroughly and shape into 20 golf–ball sized rounds.

Heat a large skillet over medium-low heat. Add the meatballs and cook, stirring gently, for 15 minutes. To check that the meat is cooked through, cut into the middle to check that there are no remaining traces of pink.

Remove the bay leaf from the sauce and serve immediately with the meatballs.

meatloaf

makes 6–8 servings

PREP TIME: 10 minutes

COOK TIME: about 1 hour
30 minutes

2 tbsp butter

1 tbsp olive oil, plus extra for
brushing

3 garlic cloves, chopped

2 carrots, finely diced

1 celery stalk, finely diced

1 onion, finely diced

1 red bell pepper, seeded and
finely diced

4 large white mushrooms, finely
diced

1 tsp dried thyme

2 tsp finely chopped rosemary

1 tsp Worcestershire sauce

1/3 cup ketchup

1/2 tsp cayenne pepper

2 1/2 lbs ground beef, chilled

2 large eggs, beaten

salt and pepper

1 cup fresh breadcrumbs

2 tbsp packed brown sugar

1 tbsp Dijon mustard

Melt the butter with the oil and garlic in a large skillet. Add the vegetables and cook over medium heat, stirring frequently, for 10 minutes, until most of the moisture has evaporated.

Remove from the heat and stir in the herbs, Worcestershire sauce, 1/4 cup of the ketchup and the cayenne pepper. Let cool.

Preheat the oven to 325°F. Brush a loaf pan with oil.

Put the beef into a large bowl and gently break it up with your fingertips. Add the vegetable mixture and eggs, season with salt and pepper, and mix gently with your fingers. Add the breadcrumbs and mix.

Transfer the meatloaf mixture to the loaf pan. Smooth the surface and bake in the preheated oven for 30 minutes.

Meanwhile, make a glaze by beating together the sugar, the remaining 2 tbsp of ketchup, the mustard and a pinch of salt.

Remove the meatloaf from the oven and spread the glaze evenly over the top. Return to the oven and bake for a further 35–45 minutes. To check the meatloaf is cooked through, cut into the middle to check that the meat is no longer pink. Any juices that run out should be clear and piping hot with visible steam rising. Remove from the oven and let rest for at least 15 minutes.

chicken pot pies

makes 6 servings

PREP TIME: 20 minutes
COOK TIME: 1 hour 20 minutes

1 tbsp olive oil

3 cups sliced white button mushrooms

1 onion, finely chopped

6 carrots, sliced

2 celery stalks, sliced

4 cups cold chicken stock

6 tbsp butter

½ cup all-purpose flour, plus extra for dusting

2 lbs boneless, skinless chicken breasts, cut into 1-inch cubes

⅔ cup frozen peas

1 tsp chopped fresh thyme

salt and pepper

2 sheets store-bought pie dough

1 large egg, lightly beaten

Preheat the oven to 400°F. Heat the oil in a large saucepan. Add the mushrooms and onion and cook over medium heat, stirring frequently, for 8 minutes until golden.

Add the carrots, celery and half the stock and bring to a boil. Reduce the heat to low and simmer for 12–15 minutes, until the vegetables are almost tender.

Meanwhile, melt the butter in a separate large saucepan over medium heat. Beat in the flour and cook, stirring continuously, for 4 minutes. Gradually beat in the remaining stock, then reduce the heat to medium-low and simmer, stirring, until thick. Stir in the vegetable mixture and add the chicken, peas and thyme.

Simmer, stirring continuously, for 5 minutes. Taste and adjust the seasoning, adding salt and pepper, if needed. Divide the mixture between 6 large ramekins.

Roll out the dough on a floured surface and cut out 6 circles, each 1 inch larger than the diameter of the ramekins. Place the dough circles on top of the filling, then crimp the edges. Cut a small cross in the center of each circle.

Put the ramekins on a baking sheet and brush the tops with beaten egg. Bake in the preheated oven for 35–40 minutes, until golden-brown and bubbling.

Let stand for 15 minutes before serving.

beef enchiladas

makes 18

PREP TIME: 35 minutes
COOK TIME: 1 hour 15 minutes

1 tbsp vegetable oil, plus extra for brushing

1 onion, finely chopped

2 fresh green chiles, seeded and chopped

12 oz ground beef

1 cup shredded cheddar cheese

18 tortillas

chopped fresh cilantro, to garnish

Piquant tomato sauce

2 tbsp butter

2 tbsp olive oil

1 onion, finely chopped

2 garlic cloves, finely chopped

1 fresh green chile, seeded and chopped

1 (14.5-oz) can diced tomatoes

2 tbsp tomato paste

brown sugar, to taste

1 tsp dried oregano

1/2 tsp cayenne pepper

salt and pepper

1/2 cup heavy cream

Heat the vegetable oil in a skillet. Add the onion and chiles and cook over low heat, stirring occasionally, for 5 minutes. Add the beef, increase the heat to medium, and cook, stirring frequently and breaking it up with the spoon, for 8–10 minutes, until evenly browned. Remove the skillet from the heat and stir in half the cheese.

To make the piquant tomato sauce, melt the butter with the olive oil in a saucepan. Add the onion, garlic and chile and cook over medium heat, stirring occasionally, for 5–8 minutes, until the onion is golden-brown. Stir in the tomatoes, tomato paste, sugar, oregano and cayenne pepper and season with salt and pepper. Increase the heat to medium and bring to a boil. Reduce the heat, stir in the cream, and simmer, stirring occasionally, for 15–20 minutes, until thickened. Remove from the heat and let cool slightly.

Meanwhile, preheat the oven to 350°F. Heat a skillet and brush with vegetable oil. One at a time, dip the tortillas in the sauce, shake off any excess, and cook in the skillet for 30 seconds on each side. Transfer to a large plate, put 1 tbsp of the meat mixture in the center, and roll up.

Put the filled tortillas, seam side down, in a large ovenproof dish and pour the remaining sauce over them. Sprinkle with the remaining cheese and bake in the preheated oven for 15–20 minutes.

Garnish with cilantro and serve.

June Shannon
Here Comes Honey Boo Boo

chicken and noodle casserole

makes 4–6 servings

PREP TIME: 1 minute
COOK TIME: 10 minutes

6 bonelesss chicken breasts (cooked)

1 large can of cream of chicken soup

2 cups milk

6 to 12 eggs (boiled)

1 large bag no-yolk noodles

Cut the cooked chicken breasts into pieces and add to a deep pan.

Pour the chicken soup into the pan and add the milk. Heat the mixture until it bubbles and is heated through.

Cook the noodles according to the instructions on the package and add to the pan.

Chop the eggs into pieces and scatter over the chicken and noodles. Mix and serve immediately.

The kids love this recipe, the more eggs the better, just watch out for the gas attack later!

baked ham

makes 6 servings

PREP TIME: 10 minutes
COOK TIME: 1 hour 30 minutes

3 lbs boneless ham
2 tbsp Dijon mustard
½ cup turbinado brown sugar
½ tsp ground cinnamon
½ tsp ground ginger
18 whole cloves
store-bought orange–red currant
sauce, to serve

Place the ham in a large pot, cover with cold water, and slowly bring to a boil over gentle heat. Cover and simmer very gently for 1 hour.

Preheat the oven to 400°F.

Remove the ham from the pan and drain. Score the fat into a diamond-shape pattern with a sharp knife.

Spread the mustard over the fat. Mix together the sugar, cinnamon and ginger on a plate and roll the ham in the mixture, pressing down well to coat evenly.

Stud the diamond shapes with cloves and place the ham in a roasting pan. Roast in the preheated oven for 20 minutes, until the glaze has turned a rich golden color.

To serve hot, let stand for 20 minutes before carving. If the ham is to be served cold, it can be cooked a day ahead. Serve with the orange–red currant sauce.

tip This dish is all about the quality of the meat, so make sure you choose a prime joint with a good covering of fat from a reliable supplier.

spicy beef tacos

makes 4 servings

PREP TIME: 25 minutes
COOK TIME: 25 minutes

2 tbsp vegetable oil
1 small onion, finely chopped
2 garlic cloves, finely chopped
1 lb ground beef
1½ tsp hot chili powder
1 tsp ground cumin
salt and pepper

8 taco shells
1 avocado
2 tbsp lemon juice
¼ head of lettuce, shredded
4 scallions, thinly sliced
2 tomatoes, peeled and diced
½ cup sour cream
1 cup shredded cheddar cheese

Heat the oil in a skillet. Add the onion and garlic and cook over low heat, stirring occasionally, for 5 minutes, until softened. Add the beef, increase the heat to medium, and cook, stirring frequently and breaking it up with a wooden spoon, for 8–10 minutes, until evenly browned. Drain off as much fat as possible.

Stir in the chili powder and cumin, season with salt and pepper, and cook over low heat, stirring frequently for an additional 8 minutes, then remove from the heat.

Heat the taco shells according to the package directions. Meanwhile, peel, pit and slice the avocado and gently toss with the lemon juice in a bowl.

Divide the lettuce, scallions, tomatoes and avocado slices among the taco shells. Add 1 tbsp of sour cream to each, then divide the beef mixture among them. Sprinkle with the cheese and serve immediately.

paprika turkey strips

makes 4 servings

PREP TIME: 10 minutes
COOK TIME: 7–10 minutes

1 lb turkey cutlets
1 tbsp paprika
1 tsp crushed coriander seeds
$^1/_2$ tsp garlic salt
$^1/_4$ tsp pepper
2 tbsp olive oil
1 red onion, sliced
3 tbsp chopped fresh cilantro
cooked rice, to serve

Cut the turkey into long strips, about $^1/_2$-inch thick.

Put the paprika, coriander seeds, garlic salt and pepper into a large bowl and mix together. Stir in 1 tbsp of the oil. Add the turkey strips and turn to coat evenly in the mixture.

Heat the remaining oil in a large skillet or wok, add the onion, and sauté, stirring, for 1 minute. Add the turkey strips and sauté, stirring over high heat for 6–8 minutes, until cooked through.

Sprinkle over the chopped cilantro and serve with rice.

fact Paprika is made by grinding dried bell peppers or chiles into a fine powder—depending on its source it can be very mild or quite strong, so choose carefully!

chicken-and-broccoli casserole

makes 4 servings

PREP TIME: 10 minutes
COOK TIME: 35 minutes

1 head of broccoli, cut into florets
3 tbsp butter
1 onion, thinly sliced
½ cups bite-size cooked chicken chunks
salt and pepper
½ cup crème fraîche or sour cream
1 cup chicken stock
½ cup fresh white breadcrumbs
½ cup shredded Swiss cheese

Preheat the oven to 400°F. Bring a saucepan of lightly salted water to a boil, add the broccoli, and cook for 5 minutes, until tender. Drain well.

Meanwhile, melt 2 tbsp of the butter in a skillet, add the onion and sauté over medium heat, stirring, for 3–4 minutes, until soft.

Layer the broccoli, onion, and chicken in a 1½-quart casserole dish and season well with salt and pepper. Pour the crème fraîche and stock over the chicken and vegetables.

Melt the remaining butter in a small saucepan and stir in the breadcrumbs. Mix with the cheese and sprinkle the mixture over the dish.

Place the dish on a baking sheet in the preheated oven and bake for 20–25 minutes, until golden-brown and bubbling. Serve hot.

variation Almonds form a perfect partnership with both chicken and broccoli—make the most of this by adding ½ cup slivered almonds to the breadcrumb-and-cheese mixture before sprinkling it over the dish.

family favorites

broiled tenderloin steaks

makes 4–6 servings

PREP TIME: 10 minutes, plus 30 minutes marinating time
COOK TIME: 15 minutes

2 tbsp olive oil

3 tbsp raspberry vinegar

1 tbsp granulated sugar

1 tbsp finely chopped fresh rosemary

4 tenderloin steaks

salt and pepper

1 small red onion, finely chopped

$\frac{1}{2}$ cup red wine

2 cups raspberries

Put the oil, vinegar, sugar and rosemary into a small bowl and mix together. Place the steaks in a nonmetallic dish and pour the vinegar mixture over the steaks. Cover and let marinate for 30 minutes.

Preheat the broiler to high. Drain the meat well, season with salt and pepper, place on the broiler rack, and cook under the preheated broiler, turning once, for 2 minutes on each side for medium–rare, and for $2\frac{1}{2}$ minutes on each side for medium. Remove from the rack and let stand for 5 minutes.

Meanwhile, put the marinade into a saucepan with the onion and bring to a boil, then cook over moderate heat, stirring, for 3–4 minutes, until the onion is soft. Add the wine, bring to a boil, and boil for 2–3 minutes, until the liquid is reduced by half. Add the raspberries and cook, stirring, for 1 minute.

Season the raspberry sauce with salt and pepper, spoon it over the steaks, and serve immediately.

thanksgiving roasted turkey

makes 4–6 servings

PREP TIME: 20 minutes
COOK TIME: 2 hours 45 minutes

1 turkey (6½ lbs)
1 onion, halved
fresh thyme sprigs
6 tbsp butter, softened
½ cup maple syrup
1 tbsp finely chopped fresh thyme
salt and pepper

1 cup chicken stock
1 tbsp lemon juice
traditional trimmings, to serve

Preheat the oven to 350°F. Put the turkey into a roasting pan and put the onion and thyme sprigs into the cavity.

Put the butter, maple syrup and chopped thyme into a bowl and mix together. Lift the turkey skin away from the breast and spread a little of the butter mixture on the meat. Replace the skin and brush more of the glaze over the skin.

Sprinkle the turkey with salt and pepper and roast in the preheated oven for 2½ hours, basting occasionally with the glaze and juices. If the skin begins to overbrown, cover it loosely with aluminum foil.

Cook until a meat thermometer inserted into the thickest part of the meat—in the inner thigh area near the breast—without touching the bone, has a reading of 180°F or until the turkey is tender and the juices run clear when the tip of a sharp knife is inserted into the thickest part of the meat. Gently pull the leg away from the body; the leg should give and no traces of pink or blood should remain. Remove from the oven, cover with foil, and let rest for about 20 minutes before carving.

Skim any fat from the pan juices and stir in the stock and lemon juice. Bring to a boil and boil until slightly reduced. Season with salt and pepper.

Serve the turkey with the gravy and trimmings.

family favorites

classic pasta dishes

chicken with creamy penne

makes 2 servings

PREP TIME: 10 minutes
COOK TIME: 20 minutes

7 oz dried penne

1 tbsp olive oil

2 boneless, skinless chicken breasts

¼ cup dry white wine

1 cup frozen peas

5 tbsp heavy cream

salt

4–5 tbsp chopped fresh parsley, to garnish

Bring a large saucepan of lightly salted water to a boil. Add the penne and cook for about 8–10 minutes, until tender but still firm to the bite.

Meanwhile, heat the oil in a skillet, add the chicken, and cook over medium heat for about 4 minutes on each side.

Pour in the wine and cook over high heat until it has almost evaporated.

Drain the pasta. Add the peas, cream and pasta to the skillet and season with salt. Cover and simmer for 2 minutes.

Garnish with parsley and serve.

variation Replace the wine with an equal quantity of Marsala for a richer, sweeter flavor.

classic pasta dishes

fusilli with zucchini and lemon

makes 4 servings

PREP TIME: 15 minutes
COOK TIME: 30 minutes

6 tbsp olive oil

1 small onion, thinly sliced

2 garlic cloves, finely chopped

2 tbsp chopped fresh rosemary

1 tbsp chopped fresh flat-leaf parsley

1 lb small zucchini, cut into 1-inch strips

finely grated zest of 1 lemon

salt and pepper

1 lb dried fusilli

¼ cup freshly grated Parmesan cheese, to serve

Heat the oil in a large skillet over medium-low heat. Add the onion and cook gently, stirring occasionally, for about 10 minutes, until golden.

Increase the heat to medium-high. Add the garlic, rosemary and parsley. Cook for a few seconds, stirring.

Add the zucchini and lemon zest. Cook for 5–7 minutes, stirring occasionally, until just tender. Season to taste with salt and pepper. Remove from the heat.

Bring a large pot of lightly salted water to a boil. Add the pasta, return to a boil, and cook for 8–10 minutes, or until tender but still firm to the bite.

Drain the pasta and transfer to a warmed serving dish.

Briefly reheat the zucchini sauce. Pour over the pasta and toss well to mix.

Sprinkle with Parmesan cheese and serve immediately.

pasta pesto

makes 4 servings

PREP TIME: 10 minutes
COOK TIME: about 10 minutes

Pesto

2 garlic cloves

3 tbsp pine nuts

salt

**3 cups fresh basil leaves,
plus extra to garnish**

$^1/_2$ cup olive oil

**$^2/_3$ cup freshly grated Parmesan
cheese**

1 lb dried tagliatelle pasta

salt

To make the pesto, put the garlic, pine nuts and a pinch of salt into a food processor and process briefly. Add the basil and process to a paste.

With the motor still running, gradually add the oil. Scrape into a bowl and beat in the Parmesan cheese. Season with salt.

Bring a large, heavy pot of lightly salted water to a boil. Add the tagliatelle, bring back to a boil, and cook according to the package directions, until tender but still firm to the bite.

Drain well, return to the saucepan, and toss with half the pesto.

Divide among warm serving dishes and top with the remaining pesto. Garnish with basil and serve immediately.

variation Think pesto, and you probably think basil—in fact, pesto can be made using a variety of different leaves, each giving a very different flavor to the pesto. Add something peppery to the pesto in this pasta dish by replacing the basil leaves with an equal quantity of arugula.

spaghetti and meat sauce

makes 4 servings

PREP TIME: 10 minutes
COOK TIME: 40 minutes

2 tbsp olive oil

1 large onion, chopped

1 lb ground beef

1 green bell pepper, seeded and chopped

1 garlic clove, crushed

$^2/_3$ cup red wine or beef stock

1 (14.5-oz) can diced tomatoes

2 tbsp tomato paste

1 tbsp dried oregano

8 oz spaghetti

salt and pepper

freshly grated Parmesan cheese, to serve

Heat the oil in a large saucepan over high heat.

Add the onion and ground beef and cook, stirring until lightly browned with no remaining traces of pink. Stir in the green bell pepper and garlic. Add the wine, tomatoes, tomato paste and oregano. Bring to a boil and boil rapidly for 2 minutes.

Reduce the heat, cover, and simmer for 20 minutes, stirring occasionally.

Meanwhile, bring a large pot of lightly salted water to a boil, add the spaghetti, bring back to a boil, and cook according to the package directions, until tender but still firm to the bite.

Drain in a colander and return to the pan. Season the sauce with salt and pepper, then stir into the spaghetti.

Serve immediately, with Parmesan cheese.

lasagna

makes 4 servings

PREP TIME: 20 minutes

COOK TIME: 1 hour 15 minutes

2 tbsp olive oil

2 oz pancetta, chopped

1 onion, chopped

1 garlic clove, finely chopped

8 oz fresh ground beef

2 celery stalks, chopped

2 carrots, chopped

salt and pepper

pinch of sugar

1/2 tsp dried oregano

1 (14.5-oz) can diced tomatoes

2 tsp Dijon mustard

2 cups store-bought alfredo sauce

8 oz oven-ready lasagna noodles

1 1/2 cups freshly grated Parmesan cheese, plus extra for sprinkling

Preheat the oven to 375°F. Heat the oil in a large, heavy saucepan. Add the pancetta and cook over medium heat, stirring occasionally, for 3 minutes.

Add the onion and garlic and cook, stirring occasionally, for 5 minutes, or until soft. Add the ground beef and cook, breaking it up with a wooden spoon, until brown all over with no remaining traces of pink. Stir in the celery and carrots and cook for 5 minutes.

Season with salt and pepper. Add the sugar, oregano and tomatoes with their juices. Bring to a boil, reduce the heat, and simmer for 30 minutes. Meanwhile, stir the mustard into the cheese sauce.

In a large, rectangular ovenproof dish, make alternate layers of meat sauce, lasagna noodles and Parmesan cheese.

Pour the cheese sauce over the layers, covering them completely, and sprinkle with Parmesan cheese. Bake in the preheated oven for 30 minutes, or until golden-brown and bubbling.

Serve immediately.

classic pasta dishes

macaroni and cheese

makes 4 servings

PREP TIME: about 40 minutes
COOK TIME: 5 minutes

9 oz macaroni

4 tbsp butter, plus extra for cooking the pasta

2¹/₂ cups milk

¹/₂ tsp grated nutmeg

¹/₂ cup all-purpose flour

³/₄ cup grated sharp cheddar cheese

³/₄ cup grated Parmesan cheese

salt and pepper

Cook the macaroni according to the package directions. Remove from the heat, drain, add a small pat of butter to keep it soft, return to the saucepan, and cover to keep warm.

Put the milk and nutmeg into a separate saucepan over low heat and heat until warm, but don't boil. Melt the butter in a heavy-bottom saucepan over low heat, add the flour, and stir to make a roux. Cook gently for 2 minutes. Add the milk a little at a time, whisking it into the roux, then cook for 10–15 minutes to make a loose sauce.

Add three-quarters of the cheddar cheese and Parmesan cheese and stir through until they have melted in, season with salt and pepper, and remove from the heat.

Preheat the broiler to high. Put the macaroni into a shallow, heatproof baking dish, then pour the sauce over. Scatter the remaining cheeses over the top and place the dish under the preheated broiler. Broil until the cheeses begin to brown, then serve.

penne in tomato sauce with two cheeses

makes 4 servings

PREP TIME: 20 minutes
COOK TIME: 35 minutes

Tomato sauce

2 tbsp butter

2 tbsp olive oil

2 shallots, finely chopped

2 garlic cloves, finely chopped

1 celery stalk, finely chopped

1 (14.5-oz) can diced tomatoes

2 tbsp tomato paste

brown sugar, to taste

1 tsp dried oregano

½ cup water

salt and pepper

1 lb penne pasta

1 cup diced Fontina, Gouda, or Muenster cheese

⅔ cup freshly grated Parmesan cheese

For the tomato sauce, melt the butter with the oil in a saucepan. Add the shallots, garlic and celery and cook over low heat, stirring occasionally, for 5 minutes, until softened. Stir in the tomatoes, tomato paste, sugar, oregano and water and season with salt and pepper. Increase the heat to medium and bring to a boil, then reduce the heat and simmer, stirring occasionally, for 15–20 minutes, until thickened.

Meanwhile, bring a large, heavy pot of lightly salted water to a boil. Add the penne, bring back to a boil and cook according to the package directions, until just tender but still firm to the bite. Drain and return to the pan.

Add the tomato sauce and the cheeses to the pasta and toss well over low heat until the cheeses have melted. Transfer to a serving dish and serve immediately.

tip Try Grana Padano instead of Parmesan—it's produced in the same region of Italy as its better-known rival, and is lower in salt, lower in fat and cheaper.

classic pasta dishes

Randy Fenoli
Say Yes to the Dress and *Randy Knows Best*

I love making this because it's so easy to make and only uses 4 basic ingredients. I made this dish once for a "pot luck" luncheon at Kleinfeld and all the ladies were asking me for the recipe!

lemon capellini

makes 4–6 servings

PREP TIME: 10 minutes

COOK TIME: 5 minutes

3 tbsp lemon zest

³/₄ cup freshly squeezed lemon juice (approximately 3-4 lemons)

1 pint (2 cups) grape tomatoes

2 cups fresh basil leaves, loosely packed (yields ¹/₂ cup chiffonade)

¹/₄ cup plus 2 tsp kosher salt

1 lb thin spaghetti (I use Barilla)

¹/₂ tsp olive oil or vegetable oil

¹/₄ tsp freshly cracked black pepper

Wash and dry lemons. Using a microplane, zest lemons to yield approximately 3 tablespoons lemon zest. Set aside.

Once you've zested the lemons, slice them in half and juice them. (I have a juice press that I love to use for this). Set juice aside.

Wash and gently dry grape tomatoes and slice in half lengthwise. Set aside.

Wash basil leaves and dry using a salad spinner or paper towels and chiffonade. (To chiffonade, stack the basil leaves one on top of the other to form a stack. "Roll" stack into what looks like a cigar and thinly slice into confetti like strips). Set aside.

In very large pot, fill two-thirds full of water and bring to a rolling boil. Slowly add ¹/₄ cup of kosher salt to season water, add thin spaghetti and cook until al dente (firm to the bite), approximately 5 minutes. Do not overcook pasta.

When pasta is ready, immediately rinse with very cold water to stop cooking process. Once the spaghetti is cooled, drain thoroughly and pour into a large mixing bowl.

Drizzle ¹/₂ tsp olive oil over pasta and toss with tongs to ensure it doesn't stick.

Add in remaining ingredients (kosher salt, black pepper, lemon zest, lemon juice, grape tomatoes and basil). Toss thoroughly and serve.

This is best eaten at room temperature but will keep for a couple days in the refrigerator.

classic pasta dishes

pasta arrabbiata

makes 4 servings

PREP TIME: 10 minutes
COOK TIME: about 1 hour

$\frac{1}{3}$ cup extra-virgin olive oil

8 plum tomatoes, diced

salt and pepper

$\frac{2}{3}$ cup dry white wine

1 tbsp sun-dried tomato pesto

2 fresh red chiles

2 garlic cloves, finely chopped

$\frac{1}{4}$ cup chopped fresh
flat-leaf parsley

14 oz penne pasta

fresh Pecorino Romano
shavings, to garnish

Heat the oil in a skillet over high heat until almost smoking. Add the tomatoes and cook, stirring frequently, for 2–3 minutes.

Reduce the heat to low and cook for about 20 minutes. Season with salt and pepper. Using a wooden spoon, press through a nonmetallic strainer into a saucepan.

Add the wine, tomato pesto, whole chiles and garlic to the pan and bring to a boil. Reduce the heat and simmer gently, then remove the chiles. Check and adjust the seasoning, adding the chiles back in for a hotter sauce, then stir in half the parsley.

Meanwhile, bring a large pot of lightly salted water to a boil. Add the pasta, bring back to a boil, and cook according to the package directions, or until tender but still firm to the bite. Add the sauce to the pasta and toss to coat.

Sprinkle with the remaining parsley, garnish with cheese shavings, and serve immediately.

spaghetti and meatballs

makes 4 servings

PREP TIME: 30 minutes

COOK TIME: about 1 hour 30 minutes

2 tbsp olive oil, plus extra for greasing

1 onion, finely chopped

4 garlic cloves, finely chopped

2 tsp salt, plus a pinch of salt

1/2 tsp dried Italian seasoning

1/2 loaf day-old Italian bread, crust removed

1/4 cup milk

2 lbs lean ground beef, well chilled

1 tsp pepper

2 extra-large eggs, beaten

1/3 cup chopped fresh flat-leaf parsley

3/4 cup freshly grated Parmesan cheese, plus extra to serve

6 cups marinara sauce, or other store-bought pasta sauce

1 cup water

1 lb spaghetti, cooked according to the package directions and drained

Heat the oil in a skillet over medium-low heat and add the onion, garlic and a pinch of salt. Sweat for 6–7 minutes, until soft and golden. Turn off the heat, stir in the dried herbs, and let cool to room temperature.

Tear the bread into small chunks and place in a food processor (work in batches, depending on the size of the machine). Pulse to make fine breadcrumbs—you'll need 2 cups. Add the crumbs to a bowl and toss with the milk to moisten. Let rest for 10 minutes.

Put the beef, 2 tsp of salt, pepper, eggs, parsley, cheese, breadcrumbs and the cooled onion mixture into a large mixing bowl, and use your hands to combine.

Preheat the oven to 375°F. Grease a baking sheet, then wet your hands and roll pieces of the mixture into golf ball–sized meatballs. Arrange the meatballs on the prepared baking sheet and bake in the preheated oven for 20 minutes.

Add the pasta sauce and water to a large pot and bring to a simmer. Add the cooked meatballs to the sauce. Reduce the heat to very low, cover, and simmer gently for 45 minutes.

Place the cooked spaghetti in a large pasta bowl. Ladle some of the sauce over the pasta and toss to coat. Serve the spaghetti in warmed bowls, topped with the meatballs, sauce and cheese.

lemon turkey with spinach

makes 4 servings

PREP TIME: 30 minutes, plus 30 minutes marinating time
COOK TIME: 10 minutes

1 tbsp soy sauce

1 tbsp white-wine vinegar

1 tsp cornstarch

1 tsp finely grated lemon zest

1/2 tsp finely ground black pepper

1 lb turkey cutlets, cut into strips

1 tbsp vegetable oil

6 scallions, finely sliced

1/2 lemon, peeled and thinly sliced

1 garlic clove, finely chopped

1 (12-oz) package fresh spinach, washed, drained and coarsely chopped

3 tbsp chopped fresh flat-leaf parsley

sprigs of fresh flat-leaf parsley, to garnish

cooked pasta, such as tagliatelle, to serve

To make the marinade, put the soy sauce, vinegar, cornstarch, lemon zest and black pepper in a bowl and mix thoroughly. Add the turkey and stir to coat. Cover with plastic wrap and marinate in the refrigerator for 30 minutes.

Heat the oil in a large preheated wok or skillet. Add the turkey and marinade and cook over medium heat for 2–3 minutes, or until the turkey is opaque.

Add the scallions, lemon slices and garlic and cook for another 2–3 minutes. Stir in the spinach and parsley and cook until the spinach is just wilted.

Remove from the heat and spoon the mixture over the cooked pasta. Garnish with sprigs of parsley and serve.

tip For a really fresh flavor, use whole fresh baby spinach leaves and add them after the parsley—they will begin to wilt almost as soon as they come in contact with the heat.

spaghetti with fresh pea pesto

makes 4 servings

PREP TIME: 10 minutes
COOK TIME: about 15 minutes

Pea pesto
2 cups shelled fresh peas
¹⁄₃ cup extra-virgin olive oil
2 garlic cloves, crushed
1 cup freshly grated Parmesan cheese, plus extra, shaved, to serve
³⁄₄ cup blanched almonds, chopped
pinch of sugar
salt and pepper

1¹⁄₂ cups shelled fava beans
1 lb spaghetti

To make the pea pesto, cook the peas in a saucepan of boiling water for 2–3 minutes, until just tender. Drain and transfer to a food processor. Add the oil, garlic and grated Parmesan cheese and process to a coarse paste. Add the almonds and process again. Add the sugar and season with salt and pepper. Set aside.

Blanch the fava beans in a saucepan of lightly salted boiling water until just tender. Drain and let cool. Peel off the skins.

Bring a large, heavy pot of lightly salted water to a boil. Add the spaghetti, bring back to a boil, and cook according to the package directions, until just tender but still firm to the bite. Drain, stir in the fava beans, and toss with the pesto. Add a good coarse grinding of pepper and serve with Parmesan cheese shavings.

classic pasta dishes

chicken fettuccine alfredo

makes 2 servings

PREP TIME: 10 minutes

COOK TIME: about 45 minutes

2 large boneless, skinless chicken breasts

2 cups low-sodium chicken broth

2 cups heavy cream

4 cloves garlic, very finely minced

2 large egg yolks

1/4 cup chopped flat-leaf Italian parsley

2 cups freshly grated Parmigiano-Reggiano cheese, plus more for serving

salt and freshly ground black pepper, to taste

1 lb fettuccine

Bring the chicken breasts and broth to a simmer in a medium saucepan over medium heat. Cover, reduce the heat to low, and simmer for 12 minutes. Turn off the heat, and let sit in the hot broth for 15 minutes. When the chicken has cooled, cut into thin slices and reserve.

Bring a large pot of lightly salted water to boil.

Bring the chicken broth back to a boil over high heat. Cook until broth has reduced by half. Add the cream and garlic. When the mixture comes to a simmer, reduce the heat to low.

Beat the egg yolks in a small bowl. Slowly whisk in 1/2 cup of the hot cream mixture to warm the eggs. Turn off the heat, and whisk egg mixture into the cream sauce. Stir in the parsley and 1 cup of the cheese. Season with salt and freshly ground black pepper, to taste. Stir in sliced chicken. Cover, and reserve.

Boil the fettuccine in the salted water, according to package directions. Drain well, but do not rinse. Quickly return pasta back into the pot, and pour over the sauce. Stir well, cover, and let sit 1 minute. Remove the cover, stir in last cup of cheese, and let sit for 1 more minute. Serve hot topped with additional grated cheese.

fact This rich, creamy pasta sauce was invented almost a century ago by Roman chef Alfredo di Lello, who named it after himself and his popular restaurant, the Alfredo.

classic pasta dishes

garlic shrimp angel hair

makes 4 servings

PREP TIME: 20 minutes

COOK TIME: about 1 hour

2 lbs raw shrimp, peeled and deveined, shells reserved

3 tbsp butter

3 cups water

¼ cup olive oil

salt, to taste

¼ cup freshly minced garlic

½ cup diced tomatoes

½ cup heavy cream

1 (14 oz) package dry angel-hair pasta

1 lemon, juiced

¼ tsp red chili flakes, or to taste

3 tbsp chopped flat-leaf Italian parsley

6 lemon wedges, optional

To make the shrimp stock: Place the shrimp shells in a saucepan, along with 1 tbsp of butter, over medium heat. Sauté the shells for about 4 minutes, then add 3 cups of water. Bring to a simmer, reduce heat to low, and simmer for 25 minutes. Strain and reserve stock until needed.

Bring a large pot of lightly salted water to a boil.

Heat the olive oil in a large skillet over high heat. Season the shrimp with salt. As soon as the oil in the pan is hot and begins to shimmer, add the shrimp and cook for 3 to 4 minutes, until they just turn pink. Remove to a bowl with a slotted spoon, leaving the olive oil in the pan. Reserve the shrimp until needed.

Add 2 tbsp of butter to the skillet and cook the garlic over medium-low heat for about 2 minutes. Do not brown the garlic. Add the tomatoes, shrimp stock and cream. Turn the heat to high, and bring the mixture to a boil, scraping the bottom with a wooden spoon to release any caramelized bits. Cook until reduced by half, about 10 minutes. Turn the heat down to low, and keep warm until needed.

Cook the angel-hair pasta 1 minute less than the package instructions. Drain into a colander. While the pasta is draining, add the shrimp to the sauce, along with the lemon juice, chili flakes and parsley. The shrimp will only take a few minutes to heat through.

Transfer the pasta back into the pot, and pour over the shrimp and sauce. Stir to combine, and let sit for 1 minute to absorb the sauce. Taste for salt, and then use tongs to divide the angel hair between the 6 plates. Using a spoon, divide the shrimp and sauce over the top of the pasta. Serve hot with lemon wedges, if desired.

on the side

roasted vegetables

makes 4–6 servings

PREP TIME: 15 minutes

COOK TIME: about 1 hour

3 parsnips, cut into 2-inch chunks

4 baby turnips, cut into quarters (optional)

3 carrots, cut into 2-inch chunks

1 lb. butternut squash, cut into 2-inch chunks

1 lb. sweet potatoes, cut into 2-inch chunks

2 garlic cloves, finely chopped

2 tbsp chopped fresh rosemary, plus extra to garnish

2 tbsp chopped fresh thyme, plus extra to garnish

2 tsp chopped fresh sage, plus extra to garnish

3 tbsp olive oil

salt and pepper

Preheat the oven to 425°F. Arrange all the vegetables in a single layer in a large roasting pan.

Sprinkle with the garlic and the herbs. Pour the oil over the vegetables and season well with salt and pepper.

Toss together all the ingredients until they are well mixed and coated with the oil. If you have time you can let them marinate so the flavors are absorbed.

Roast the vegetables at the top of the preheated oven for 50–60 minutes, until they are cooked and browned. Turn the vegetables over halfway through the cooking time.

Serve with a good handful of fresh herbs sprinkled over the top and a final sprinkling of salt and pepper.

variation This delicious winter dish makes the most of a variety of root vegetables—you can make a mouthwatering summer version with chopped garlic and bell peppers, eggplant, zucchini and fennel cut into chunks. Cook in exactly the same way, then scatter over torn fresh basil leaves.

on the side

corn on the cob with blue-cheese dressing

makes 6 servings

PREP TIME: 10 minutes
COOK TIME: 20 minutes

5 oz blue cheese
²/₃ cup cottage cheese
½ cup Greek yogurt
salt and pepper

6 fresh ears of corn

Heat the grill. Crumble the blue cheese into a bowl. Beat with a wooden spoon until creamy. Stir in the cottage cheese until thoroughly blended. Gradually stir in the yogurt and season with salt and pepper. Cover with plastic wrap and let chill in the refrigerator while you prepare the corn.

Fold back the husks on each corn cob and remove the silk. Smooth the husks back into place. Cut out 6 rectangles of aluminum foil, each large enough to enclose an ear of corn. Wrap the ears of corn in the foil.

Cook the ears of corn on the grill for 15–20 minutes, turning frequently. Unwrap the corn and discard the foil. Peel back the husk on one side of each and trim off with a sharp knife. Serve with the blue-cheese dressing.

mashed yams with parsley butter

makes 4 servings

PREP TIME: 10 minutes
COOK TIME: 25 minutes

4 tbsp butter, softened
2 tbsp chopped fresh parsley
2 lbs yams, peeled
salt

Put half the butter into a bowl with the parsley and beat together. Turn out onto a square of aluminum foil or plastic wrap, shape into a block, and chill in the refrigerator until firm.

Cut the yams into even chunks. Bring a large saucepan of lightly salted water to a boil, add the yams, bring back to a boil, and cook, covered, for 15–20 minutes, until tender.

Drain the yams well, then cover the pan with a clean dish towel and let stand for 2 minutes. Mash with a potato masher until fluffy.

Add the reserved butter to the yams and stir in evenly, season to taste with salt. Spoon the mashed yams into a serving dish and serve hot, topped with chunks of parsley butter.

variation Almost any winter root vegetable can be cooked in this way, with equally delicious results—try butternut squash, turnips or parsnips, or parsnips cooked with an equal quantity of carrots.

parker house rolls

makes 12 rolls

PREP TIME: about 1 hour
COOK TIME: 12–15 minutes

1/2 cup milk

1/4 cup water

5 tbsp butter, softened, plus extra for brushing

2 1/2 cups bread flour, plus extra for dusting

2 1/4 tsp active dry yeast

1 tbsp sugar

1/2 tsp salt

1 extra-large egg, beaten

vegetable oil, for greasing

Put the milk, water and 2 tbsp of the butter into a small saucepan and heat to 110–120°F.

Put the flour, yeast, sugar and salt into a large bowl, stir, and make a well in the center. Slowly pour in 6 tbsp of the milk mixture, then add the egg and beat, drawing in the flour from the side. Add the remaining milk, tbsp by tbsp, until a soft dough forms.

Grease a bowl and set aside. Turn out the dough onto a lightly floured counter and knead for 8–10 minutes, until smooth and elastic. Shape the dough into a ball, roll it around in the greased bowl, cover with plastic wrap, and set aside for 1 hour, or until doubled in size.

Turn out the dough onto a lightly floured counter and punch down. Cover with the upturned bowl and let rest for 10 minutes. Meanwhile, preheat the oven to 400°F and dust a baking sheet with flour. Melt the remaining butter in a small saucepan over medium heat.

Lightly flour a rolling pin and use to roll out the dough to a thickness of 1/4-inch. Using a floured 3 1/4-inch round cookie cutter, cut out 12 circles, rerolling the trimmings, if necessary. Brush the middle of a dough circle with butter. Use a floured chopstick or pencil to make an indentation just off center, then fold along that indentation and pinch the edges together to seal. Place on the prepared baking sheet, cover with a dish towel, and let rise while you shape the remaining rolls.

Lightly brush the tops of the rolls with butter and bake in the preheated oven for 12–15 minutes, until the rolls are golden brown and the bottoms sound hollow when tapped. Transfer to a wire rack to cool. Serve warm or at room temperature.

roasted potatoes

makes 6 servings

PREP TIME: 10 minutes

COOK TIME: 1 hour

3 lbs large russet potatoes, peeled and cut into even chunks

3 tbsp drippings, goose fat, duck fat or olive oil

salt

Preheat the oven to 425°F.

Bring a large saucepan of lightly salted water to a boil, add the potatoes, and cook over medium heat, covered, for 5–7 minutes. (They will still be firm.) Remove from the heat.

Meanwhile, add the drippings to a baking dish and place in the preheated oven.

Drain the potatoes well and return them to the pan. Cover with the lid and firmly shake the pan so that the surface of the potatoes is roughened to help give a much crisper texture.

Remove the baking dish from the oven and carefully put the potatoes into the hot fat. Baste them to ensure they are all coated with the fat.

Roast at the top of the oven for 45–50 minutes, until they are browned all over and thoroughly crisp. Turn and baste again only once during the cooking process or the crunchy edges will be destroyed.

Carefully transfer the potatoes from the baking dish into a warmed serving dish. Sprinkle with a little salt and serve immediately.

Jen and Bill Klein
The Little Couple

It doesn't get much easier, better or healthier than this...when it comes to fries anyway.

crunchy sweet-potato fries without the fry

serves 2–3

■ ■ ■

PREP TIME: 10 minutes

COOK TIME: about 35 minutes

2 large sweet potatoes

4 tablespoons olive oil

2 tablespoons ground (not super coarse) sea salt

1 tablespoon ground black pepper

1 tablespoon ground red pepper

1 tablespoon garlic powder

1 tablespoon curry powder

Preheat the oven to 450°F.

Peel and rinse the sweet potatoes before drying them and cutting them into fry-shaped pieces.

Take the uncooked fries and place them in a large mixing bowl or zip-close bag. Add the olive oil to the sweet potato, coating all of the fries.

Mix all of the spices together and sprinkle over the fries, mixing regularly to ensure all fries are coated. Transfer the fries from the bowl or zip-close bag and place them on a nonstick pan in a single layer with a little space between each.

Bake for 15–20 minutes in the oven, flip them over and place back into the oven for another 10–15 minutes so they can cook evenly on all sides. The fries should be pretty crispy. You can leave them in a bit longer if you like them extra-crispy like Jen does.

Fries are better crispy, so don't make the mistake of preemptively abandoning the oven. Better to test them first.

Take them off the baking sheet and serve. You can add a dip if you like, but I think they are best just like this!

on the side

sweet-and-sour red cabbage

makes 6–8 servings

PREP TIME: 15 minutes

COOK TIME: about 15 minutes

1 head red cabbage

2 tbsp olive oil

2 onions, finely sliced

1 garlic clove, chopped

2 small apples, peeled, cored, and sliced

2 tbsp light brown sugar

½ tsp ground cinnamon

1 tsp crushed juniper berries

whole nutmeg, for grating

2 tbsp red-wine vinegar

grated zest and juice of 1 orange

salt and pepper

2 tbsp cranberry jelly

Cut the cabbage into quarters, remove and discard the central stalk, and finely shred.

Heat the oil in a large pot or Dutch oven and add the cabbage, onions, garlic and apples. Sprinkle over the sugar, cinnamon and juniper berries and grate one-quarter of the nutmeg into the pan.

Pour over the vinegar and orange juice and add the orange zest. Stir well and season with salt and pepper to taste.

Cook over medium heat, stirring occasionally, until the cabbage is just tender but still has "bite." This will take 10–15 minutes, depending on how finely the cabbage is sliced.

Stir in the cranberry jelly and add more salt and pepper, if necessary. Serve hot.

tip Add 2 teaspoons of melted butter just before the end of cooking and stir to coat the cabbage—this will give the dish a lovely glossy appearance.

mashed potatoes

makes 4 servings

PREP TIME: 10 minutes

COOK TIME: 30 minutes

2 lbs russet potatoes

4 tbsp butter

3 tbsp hot milk

salt and pepper

Peel the potatoes, placing them in cold water as you prepare the others to prevent them from turning brown.

Cut the potatoes into even chunks. Bring a large pot of lightly salted water to a boil, add the potatoes, and cook over medium heat, covered, for 20–25 minutes, until they are tender. Test with the point of a knife right to the center to avoid lumps.

Remove the pot from the heat and drain the potatoes. Return the potatoes to the hot pot and mash with a potato masher until smooth.

Add the butter and continue to mash until it is all mixed in, then add the milk.

Taste and season with salt and pepper as necessary. Serve immediately.

on the side

asparagus with lemon-butter sauce

makes 4 servings

PREP TIME: 10 minutes
COOK TIME: 10 minutes

1 lb 12 oz asparagus spears, trimmed
1 tbsp olive oil
salt and pepper

Lemon-butter sauce
juice of $\frac{1}{2}$ lemon
2 tbsp water
7 tbsp butter, cut into cubes

Preheat the oven to 400°F.

Lay the asparagus spears in a single layer on a large baking sheet. Drizzle over the oil, then season with salt and pepper to taste and roast in the preheated oven for 10 minutes, or until just tender.

Meanwhile, make the lemon-butter sauce. Pour the lemon juice into a saucepan and add the water. Heat for a minute or so, then slowly add the butter, cube by cube, stirring continuously, until it has all been incorporated. Season with pepper to taste and serve immediately with the asparagus.

variation For an unusual spin on this classic dish, serve it with an orange-butter sauce. Simply replace the lemon juice with orange juice, then stir in the grated zest of 1 orange after you've added the water.

hush puppies

makes 30–35 hush puppies

PREP TIME: 15 minutes

2 cups yellow cornmeal

½ cup all-purpose flour, sifted

1 small onion, finely chopped

1 tbsp superfine sugar

2 tsp baking powder

pinch of salt

¾ cup milk

1 large egg, beaten

corn oil, for deep-frying

Stir the cornmeal, flour, onion, sugar, baking powder and salt together in a bowl and make a well in the center.

Beat the milk and egg together in a large measuring cup, then pour into the dry ingredients and stir until a thick batter forms.

Heat at least 2 inches of oil in a deep skillet or saucepan over high heat, until the temperature reaches 350°F or until a cube of bread browns in 30 seconds.

Drop in as many spoonfuls of the batter as will fit without over-crowding the skillet and cook, stirring continuously, until the hush puppies puff up and turn golden.

Remove from the oil with a slotted spoon and drain on paper towels. Reheat the oil, if necessary, and cook the remaining batter. Serve hot.

on the side

cakes, cookies *and* bars

Buddy Valastro
Cake Boss, *Next Great Baker*
and *Bakery Go Time!*

These cupcakes have a delicious
surprise inside, a pop of raspberry jam
that offsets the chocolate incredibly.

stuffed cupcakes

makes 12 cupcakes

PREP TIME: 15 minutes
COOK TIME: 25 minutes

1 cup all-purpose flour
³/₄ cup sugar
1¹/₂ tsp baking powder
¹/₄ tsp salt
¹/₄ cup shortening
¹/₂ cup whole milk
³/₄ tsp vanilla
2 egg whites from large eggs
1 large (use egg whites for
a white cake and yolk for a
yellow cake)
1 cup raspberry jam
3 cups Chocolate-Fudge
Frosting (recipe opposite)

Preheat oven to 350°F. Line cupcake pans with paper liners.

Combine flour, sugar, baking powder, salt, shortening, milk and vanilla
in a large mixing bowl. Mix at low speed for 2 minutes. Scrape bowl.
Add egg whites and additional whites or yolks, and mix at high speed
until fluffy and smooth, approximately 2 minutes.

Fill liners one-half to two-thirds full of batter. Do not overfill. Bake
20–25 minutes or until toothpick inserted in center comes out clean.
Let cool 10 minutes in pans then remove from pan, and place on wire
racks to cool completely.

Place raspberry jam into a piping bag with a fine tip.

With a paring knife cut a cone shape into the the top of the cupcake.
Remove the cone to reveal a hole in the top of the cupcake.

Pipe about 1 tablespoon of raspberry jam into the whole of the
cupcake. Place the piece of cut-out cake back into the hole of the
cupcake.

Place chocolate-fudge frosting into a piping bag with a large star tip.
Frost the top of the cupcakes.

chocolate-fudge frosting

■ ■ ■

2$\frac{1}{2}$ cups (5 sticks) unsalted butter, softened at room temperature

5 cups confectioners' sugar

$\frac{2}{3}$ cup cocoa

1 tbsp pure vanilla extract

$\frac{1}{4}$ tsp fine sea salt

3 tbsp lukewarm water

Put the butter in the bowl of a stand mixer fitted with the paddle attachment and mix on low speed until smooth, approximately 3 minutes.

With the motor running, add the sugar, one cup at a time, only adding the next cup after the first addition is absorbed.

Stop the maching and add the cocoa, vanilla and salt. Mix on low-medium speed until completely smooth, approximately 2 minutes.

Add the water and continue to mix until light and fluffy, 2–3 minutes.

The frosting will keep for up to 2 days in an airtight container at room temperature.

frosted peanut-butter cupcakes

makes 16 cupcakes

PREP TIME: 25 minutes
COOK TIME: 25 minutes

4 tbsp butter, softened
1 cup packed light brown sugar
1 cup crunchy peanut butter
2 large eggs, lightly beaten
1 tsp vanilla extract
1 cup all-purpose flour
2 tsp baking powder
³/₄ cup milk

Frosting
1 cup cream cheese
2 tbsp butter, softened
2 cups confectioners' sugar

Preheat the oven to 350°F. Put 16 double-layer paper liners on a baking sheet.

Put the butter, sugar and peanut butter in a bowl and beat together until well mixed. Gradually add the eggs, beating well after each addition, then add the vanilla extract.

Sift in the flour and baking powder into a bowl, then use a rubber spatula to fold in, alternating with the milk.

Spoon the mixture into the paper liners and bake in the preheated oven for 25 minutes, or until well risen and golden-brown. Transfer to a wire rack and let cool.

For the frosting, put the cream cheese and butter into a large bowl and beat together until smooth. Sift in the confectioners' sugar, then beat until well mixed.

When the cupcakes are cold, spread some frosting on top of each, swirling with a butter knife. Refrigerate until ready to serve.

cakes, cookies and bars

lemon pound cake

makes 8 servings

PREP TIME: 15 minutes

COOK TIME: about 1 hour

butter, for greasing

1³/₄ cups all-purpose flour

2 tsp baking powder

1 cup sugar

4 large eggs

²/₃ cup sour cream

grated zest of 1 large lemon

¹/₄ cup lemon juice

²/₃ cup vegetable oil

Syrup

¹/₄ cup confectioners' sugar

3 tbsp lemon juice

Preheat the oven to 350°F.

Lightly grease a round springform pan and line the bottom with parchment paper.

Sift the flour and baking powder together into a mixing bowl and stir in the sugar.

In a separate bowl, whisk the eggs, sour cream, lemon zest, lemon juice and oil together.

Pour the egg mixture into the dry ingredients and mix well until evenly combined.

Pour the mixture into the prepared pan and bake in the preheated oven for 45–60 minutes, or until risen and golden-brown.

To make the syrup, mix the sugar and lemon juice together in a small pan. Stir over low heat until just beginning to bubble and turn syrupy.

As soon as the cake comes out of the oven, prick the surface all over with a fine skewer, then brush the syrup over the top. Let the cake cool completely in the pan before turning out and serving.

Katherine
Sophie

When we were little girls, one of our favorite things to make to drink were strawberry banana smoothies. So, we decided to turn our favorite summertime drink into a cupcake form using fresh strawberries and bananas and the result was delicious!

strawberry-banana cupcakes with strawberry frosting

makes 12 cupcakes

Sophie & Katherine
DC Cupcakes

PREP TIME: 10 minutes
COOK TIME: 15-20 minutes

2¹/₂ cups all-purpose flour

2¹/₂ tsp baking powder

¹/₄ tsp salt

8 tbsp unsalted butter, at room temperature

1³/₄ cups sugar

2 large eggs, at room temperature

2¹/₄ tsp pure vanilla extract

1¹/₄ cups whole milk, at room temperature

¹/₂ cup diced fresh strawberries

¹/₂ cup diced fresh ripe bananas

Frosting

4 tbsp unsalted butter, at room temperature

6 oz. cream cheese, at room temperature

¹/₄ tsp pure vanilla extract

4 cups confectioners' sugar, sifted

¹/₂ cup diced fresh strawberries

Preheat the oven to 350°F. Line a standard cupcake pan with twelve paper baking cups.

Sift together the flour, baking powder and salt on a sheet of parchment paper or wax paper and set aside.

In the bowl of a stand mixer or in a bowl with a handheld electric mixer, cream together the butter and sugar for 3 to 5 minutes, or until light and fluffy. Add the eggs one at a time, mixing slowly after each addition. Add the vanilla to the milk in a large liquid measuring cup.

Add one-third of the dry ingredients followed by one-third of the milk, and mix thoroughly. Repeat. Stop to scrape down the bowl as needed. Add the last third of dry ingredients followed by the last third of milk. Mix thoroughly. Add the diced strawberries and bananas and mix slowly until just incorporated.

Scoop the batter into the cupcake pan using a standard-size ice-cream scoop until each cup is two-thirds full. Bake for 16 to 18 minutes (start checking at 15 minutes), or until a toothpick comes out clean. Transfer the pan to a wire rack to cool completely.

For the frosting: Combine all of the ingredients in a mixer and whip together at high speed until light and airy, approximately 3 to 5 minutes. Transfer the frosting into a large piping bag fitted with a large round tip and frost each cupcake with a signature swirl. Serve and enjoy!

rich almond cake

makes 8 servings

PREP TIME: 15 minutes

COOK TIME: about 1 hour

butter, for greasing

1 cup ricotta cheese

4 large eggs, separated

1 tsp almond extract

1 cup sugar

2 cups ground almonds

finely grated zest of 1 lime

toasted slivered almonds,
to decorate

confectioners' sugar, sifted,
for dusting

Preheat the oven to 300°F. Grease and line a 9-inch round cake pan.

Beat together the ricotta, egg yolks, almond extract and sugar. Stir in the almonds and lime zest.

Whisk the egg whites in a clean bowl until they form soft peaks. Fold the whites lightly into the ricotta mixture, using a large rubber spatula.

Spread the mixture in the pan and bake in the preheated oven for 50–60 minutes, until firm and lightly browned.

Cool the cake in the pan for 10 minutes, then turn out onto a wire rack and sprinkle with slivered almonds. Leave to cool completely.

Dust with confectioners' sugar and serve.

tip This rich Italian classic will have an even more authentic fresh almond flavor if you grind the almonds yourself just before you mix the cake—just pulse them in the food processor for a few seconds until finely ground.

chocolate-chip brownies

makes 12 brownies

PREP TIME: 20 minutes
COOK TIME: 30–35 minutes

2 sticks (16 tbsp) butter,
softened, plus extra for greasing

5¹⁄₂ oz dark chocolate, broken
into pieces

1 cup self-rising flour

²⁄₃ cup superfine sugar

4 large eggs, beaten

¹⁄₂ cup chopped pistachio nuts

3¹⁄₂ oz white chocolate, roughly
chopped

confectioners' sugar, sifted,
for dusting

Preheat the oven to 350°F. Grease and line a 9-inch square baking pan.

Place the butter and dark chocolate in a heatproof bowl set over a saucepan of simmering water. Stir until melted, then let cool slightly.

Sift the flour into a separate bowl and stir in the superfine sugar.

Stir the eggs into the chocolate mixture, then pour into the flour and sugar and beat well. Stir in the nuts and white chocolate.

Pour the mixture into the prepared pan, using an offset spatula to spread evenly.

Bake in the preheated oven for 30–35 minutes, or until firm to the touch around the edges. Cool in the pan for 20 minutes, then turn out onto a wire rack to cool completely. Dust with confectioners' sugar and let cool completely.

Cut into 12 squares and serve.

Katherine
Sophie

This cupcake is one of our all time favorite recipes a the cupcakes are especially yummy when they are s warm right from the oven, even without the frostin

vanilla chocolate-chip cupcakes with vanilla chocolate-chip buttercream

makes 12 cupcakes

Sophie & Katherine
DC Cupcakes

PREP TIME: 10 minutes
COOK TIME: 15-20 minutes

2$^1/_2$ cups all-purpose flour

2$^1/_2$ tsp baking powder

$^1/_4$ tsp salt

8 tbsp unsalted butter, at room temperature

1$^3/_4$ cups sugar

2 large eggs, at room temperature

2$^1/_4$ tsp pure vanilla extract

1$^1/_4$ cups whole milk, at room temperature

$^1/_2$ cup semisweet chocolate chips

Frosting

16 tbsp unsalted butter, at room temperature

4 cups confectioners' sugar, sifted

1 tsp whole milk

1 tsp pure vanilla extract

pinch salt

1 cup semisweet chocolate chips

Preheat the oven to 350°F. Line a standard cupcake pan with 12 paper baking cups, or grease the pan with butter if not using baking cups.

Sift together the flour, baking powder and salt on a sheet of parchment paper or wax paper and set aside.

In the bowl of a stand mixer or in a bowl with a handheld electric mixer, cream together the butter and sugar for 3 to 5 minutes, or until light and fluffy. Add the eggs one at a time, mixing slowly after each addition. Add the vanilla extract to the milk in a large liquid measuring cup.

Add one-third of the dry ingredients followed by one-third of the milk, and mix thoroughly. Repeat. Add the last third of dry ingredients followed by the last third of milk. Mix slowly until fully incorporated. Add the $^1/_2$ cup of chocolate chips and mix slowly until just incorporated.

Scoop the batter into the cupcake pan using a standard-size ice-cream scoop until the cups are two-thirds full, and bake for 16 to 18 minutes (start checking at 15 minutes) or until a toothpick comes out clean. Transfer the pan to a wire rack to cool completely.

For the frosting: Combine all of the ingredients except for the chocolate chips in a mixer and whip together at high speed until light and airy, approximately 3 to 5 minutes. Transfer into a large piping bag with large round tip and frost each cupcake with a signature swirl. Add some chocolate chips, serve and enjoy!

cakes, cookies and bars

rocky road bars

makes 8 bars

PREP TIME: 20 minutes, plus
2 hours chilling time

COOK TIME: no cooking

**6 oz milk chocolate or
semisweet dark chocolate**

4 tbsp butter

**4 oz shortbread cookies, broken
into pieces**

**1½ cups white miniature
marshmallows**

¾ cup walnuts or peanuts

**confectioners' sugar, sifted,
for dusting**

Line a 7-inch square cake pan with parchment paper.

Break the chocolate into squares and place in a heatproof bowl. Set the bowl over a saucepan of gently simmering water and heat until the chocolate is melted, being careful to make sure that the bowl does not touch the water. Add the butter and stir until melted and combined. Let cool slightly.

Stir the broken cookies, marshmallows and nuts into the chocolate mixture. Pour the chocolate batter into the lined pan, pressing down with the back of a spoon. Chill in the refrigerator for at least 2 hours, or until firm.

Carefully invert out of the pan onto a cutting board. Dust with confectioners' sugar and cut into 8 pieces to serve.

variation These popular bars are simplicity itself to prepare, and the shortbread cookies give them an irresistibly rich flavor—try substituting ginger snaps for a spicy alternative.

Marissa Lopez
Winner of Season Two, TLC's
Next Great Baker

This simple cake is light and delicious. For an alternative omit the vanilla and add lemon extract and fresh lemon zest or all-spice and apples for an easy apple spice cake. For a children's party add a few drops of food coloring for a crazy colored birthday cake.

vanilla sponge cake

makes 8–10 servings

■ ■ ■

PREP TIME: 10 minutes
COOK TIME: 20-25 minutes

1½ sticks unsalted butter
2 cups sugar
6 large eggs
2 tbsp vanilla extract
¼ cup vegetable oil
2¾ cups cake flour
1 tbsp baking powder
pinch of salt

Preheat oven to 350°F and then reduce temperature to 325°F.

Grease two 8-inch pans with cooking spray, followed with an 8-inch round piece of parchment paper, then spray again.

Cream butter and sugar in a stand mixer with a paddle attachment until smooth.

Add the eggs, vanilla and oil and beat till combined, scraping the bowl.

Add all cake flour, baking powder and salt and mix until combined.

Pour evenly into the prepared pans and bake for 20-25 minutes.

Let cool before removing from the pan and store wrapped in refrigerator for one week maximum.

icebox cookies

makes about 56 cookies

■ ■ ■

PREP TIME: 15 minutes, plus
4 hours chilling time
COOK TIME: 12 minutes

2 $\frac{1}{3}$ cups all-purpose flour
2 tbsp unsweetened cocoa
$\frac{1}{2}$ tsp baking soda
1 tsp ground ginger
$\frac{1}{2}$ tsp ground cinnamon
$\frac{1}{2}$ cup molasses
$\frac{1}{4}$ cup boiling water
8 tbsp (1 stick) butter, softened
$\frac{1}{4}$ cup superfine sugar
confectioners' sugar, for dusting

Sift the flour, cocoa, baking soda, ginger and cinnamon together into a bowl, then set aside. Mix the molasses with the water and set aside.

Put the butter into a large bowl and beat with an electric mixer until creamy. Slowly add the superfine sugar and continue beating until light and fluffy. Gradually add the flour mixture, alternating it with the molasses mixture to form a soft dough.

Scrape equal amounts of the dough onto 2 pieces of plastic wrap and roll into logs, using the plastic wrap as a guide, each about 7$\frac{1}{2}$-inches long and 1$\frac{1}{2}$-inch thick. Put the dough logs in the refrigerator for 2 hours, then transfer to the freezer for at least 2 hours and up to 2 months.

When ready to bake, preheat the oven to 350°F and line 1 or 2 baking sheets (depending on how many cookies you are baking) with parchment paper. Unwrap the dough, trim the ends, and cut off $\frac{1}{4}$-inch-thick slices. Rewrap any unused dough and return to the freezer.

Place the dough slices on the prepared baking sheet(s) and bake in the preheated oven for 12 minutes. Let cool on the baking sheet(s) for 3 minutes, then transfer to wire racks, dust with confectioners' sugar, and let cool completely.

cakes, cookies and bars

I know this is my best friends favorite cake. She's known to add a peanut butter filling to make it extra tasty.

dark-chocolate cake with peanut butter

makes 10–12 servings

Marissa Lopez
Winner of Season Two, TLC's
Next Great Baker

PREP TIME: 10 minutes
COOK TIME: 28-30 minutes

3¼ cup sugar
2½ cup cake flour
1¼ cup coca powder
2¼ tsp baking powder
2¼ tsp baking soda
3 large eggs
1½ cup buttermilk
2 tbsp white vinegar
¾ cup oil
2 tsp vanilla
1¼ cup hot water

Filling
1 lb cream cheese
3 cups peanut butter
2 cups confectioner's sugar
2 tsps vanilla extract
1 cup heavy cream

Preheat the oven to 325°F and grease two 10-inch pan with cooking spray, followed with a 10-inch round piece of parchment paper, then spray again.

Mix all of the dry ingredients in a stand mixer with a whip attachment and add all liquid except the hot water.

Mix well, scraping the bowl and adding the hot water slowly.

Pour the batter evenly between the tins and bake for 28–30 minutes, until a knife inserted into the center of the cake comes out clean.

To make the filling: In the bowl of a stand mixer with paddle attachment, cream the peanut butter and cream cheese with the sugar until smooth. Add the vanilla and the heavy cream until combined.

Let the cake cool before removing from the pan. Spread half of the filling on one of the cakes and sandwich together. Use the remaining filling to frost the top of the cake.

Store in an airtight container in the refrigerator.

brown sugar–walnut loaf cake

makes 8–10 servings

PREP TIME: 25 minutes
COOK TIME: about 1 hour

3¼ cups all-purpose flour
1 tsp salt
4 sticks (1 lb) unsalted butter
2 cups firmly packed light brown sugar
1½ tsp vanilla extract
8 large eggs
2 cups toasted chopped walnuts

Preheat oven to 350°F.

Grease two 9x5x3-inch loaf pans and line with parchment paper.

Combine the flour and salt in a bowl and set aside.

Cream the butter and brown sugar with an electric mixer on high speed until pale and fluffy. Add the vanilla extract and mix thoroughly.

Lightly beat eggs and add to the butter and sugar. Mix thoroughly. Add in the flour and salt and mix well. Fold the chopped walnuts into the batter. Divide the batter between the pans.

Bake until a toothpick inserted into center of each cake comes out clean, about 65 minutes. Cool in pans on a wire rack for 30 minutes before removing.

Katherine
Sophie

Sophie & Katherine
DC Cupcakes

This recipe was inspired by our Candy Bar cupcake featured in the Halloween episode of *DC Cupcakes*. you don't like toffee or heath bar, you can always substitute with your favorite crushed up candy bars

chocolate toffee-crunch cupcakes with vanilla toffee-crunch frosting

makes 12 cupcakes

■ ■ ■

PREP TIME: 10 minutes
COOK TIME: 15-20 minutes

1¼ cups sifted all-purpose flour
½ tsp baking soda
¼ tsp salt
8 tbsp unsalted butter
1¼ cups sugar
2 large eggs
1¼ tsp pure vanilla extract
1 cup milk
½ cup crushed toffee candy-bar pieces
½ cup sifted cocoa powder

Frosting
4 tbsp unsalted butter
4 cups sifted confectioners' sugar
¼ tsp pure vanilla extract
6 oz. cream cheese
1 cup crushed toffee candy-bar pieces

Preheat the oven to 350°F. Line a cupcake pan with 12 paper baking cups and a second pan with six baking cups.

Sift together the flour, baking soda and salt in a bowl, and set aside. In the bowl of a stand mixer or in a bowl with a handheld electric mixer, cream together the butter and sugar on medium speed until light and fluffy, approximately 3 to 5 minutes. Add the eggs one at a time, mixing slowly after each addition. Combine the vanilla and milk in a large liquid measuring cup.

Add one-third of the flour mixture to the butter mixture, then gradually add one-third of the milk mixture, beating slowly until well incorporated. Add another third of the flour mixture, followed by another third of the milk mixture. Stop to scrape down the bowl as needed. Add the remaining mixture, followed by the remaining milk mixture, and beat just until combine Add the cocoa powder, beating on low speed just until incorporated.

Add the ½ cup of crushed toffee candy-bar pieces and mix until just combined. Using a standard-size ice cream scoop, fill each baking cup so that it is two-thirds full. Bake for 18 to 20 minutes (start checking at 15 minutes) or until a toothpick inserted into the center of a cupcake comes out clean. Transfer the pans to a wire rack to cool completely.

For the frosting: In the bowl of a stand mixer or in a bowl with a handheld electric mixer, mix all the ingredients except for the crushed toffee candy pieces for approximately 3 to 5 minutes, until the frosting is light and airy

Transfer the frosting to a plastic piping bag fitted with a round metal tip and frost each cupcake with a signature swirl. Garnish with a spoonful of crushed toffee candy-bar pieces, serve and enjoy!

cakes, cookies and bars

black-and-white brownies

makes 24 brownies

PREP TIME: about 25 minutes
COOK TIME: 40 minutes

Chocolate mixture

8 tbsp (1 stick) butter
2 cups semisweet chocolate pieces
6 large eggs
2¼ cups sugar
1½ cups all-purpose flour
1½ tsp baking powder
1½ tsp salt
1½ tbsp vanilla extract
1 tsp almond extract

Cream-cheese mixture

6 tbsp butter, softened
1 cup cream cheese, softened
¾ cup sugar
3 large eggs
3 tbsp all-purpose flour
1 tbsp vanilla extract

Preheat oven to 350°F.

Grease a 9 x 13–inch baking pan.

For the chocolate mixture, melt the butter and the chocolate in a heatproof bowl placed over a pan of gently simmering water. Mix well and set aside to cool.

In a separate bowl, beat the eggs and sugar until fluffy. Stir together the flour, baking powder and salt and mix into egg mixture. Mix in the melted chocolate and butter, and add the vanilla and almond extracts.

For the cream-cheese mixture, cream the butter, then add the cream cheese and sugar. Beat until fluffy and add in the eggs, then the flour and vanilla extract.

Spread half of the chocolate mixture into the pan, then spread with the cream-cheese mixture. Spoon the remaining chocolate batter on top. Swirl the two mixtures together with a knife. Bake for 40 minutes. Cool and cut into bars.

Marissa Lopez

Who can resist a delicious red velvet cake, especially when it's topped with cream-cheese frosting. The ultimate decadent delight!

red-velvet cake with cream-cheese frosting

makes 10–12 servings

PREP TIME: 10 minutes
COOK TIME: 20-25 minutes

5 cups cake flour

3 cups sugar

2 tsp baking soda

pinch of salt

4 tbsp Dutch cocoa

1³/₄ cups buttermilk

4 large eggs

3 cups vegetable oil

2 tbsp vanilla

2 tbsp vinegar

2 to 3 drops of red food coloring

Filling

1 lb cream cheese

8 oz unsalted butter (room temperature)

2 cups confectioner's sugar

Preheat the oven to 325°F and grease two 10-inch pans with cooking spray, followed with a 10-inch round piece of parchment paper, then spray again.

In the bowl of a stand mixer with a whip attachment whisk all the wet ingredients with the dry ingredients, adding the food coloring last. (I suggest KopyKake Flow Paste red food coloring as it never fades when baked.)

Add the cake mixture evenly into the prepared pans and bake for 20-25 minutes until a knife inserted into the center of the cake comes out clean.

Let cool and remove from pan.

To make the cream-cheese filling: In a mixer with a paddle attachment, beat all the ingredients until smooth. Spread half of the filling on one of the cakes and sandwich together. Use the remaining filling to frost the top of the cake.

Store in an airtight container in the refrigerator.

pies *and* desserts

ginger baked alaska

makes 4 servings

PREP TIME: 20 minutes, plus freezing time

COOK TIME: 5 minutes

¼ cup golden raisins

3 tbsp dark rum

4 slices ginger cake

4 scoops vanilla ice cream or rum-raisin ice cream

3 large egg whites

1 cup granulated or superfine sugar

Preheat the oven to 450°F. Mix the golden raisins with the rum in a small bowl.

Place the cake slices, spaced well apart, on a baking sheet. Scatter a spoonful of the soaked golden raisins on top of each slice. Place a scoop of ice cream in the center of each slice, then transfer to the freezer until solid.

Meanwhile, whip the egg whites in a large bowl until soft peaks form. Gradually whip the sugar into the egg whites, a spoonful at a time, until the mixture forms stiff peaks.

Remove the ice cream–topped cake slices from the freezer and spoon the meringue over the top, spreading to cover the ice cream completely.

Bake in the preheated oven for about 5 minutes, until starting to brown.

Serve immediately.

new york cheesecake

serves 6–8

PREP TIME: 25 minutes

COOK TIME: 55 minutes, plus 2 hours setting time

8 tbsp (1 stick) butter

1¹/₂ cups finely crushed graham crackers

1 tbsp granulated sugar

4 cups cream cheese, softened

1¹/₄ cups superfine sugar

2 tbsp all-purpose flour

1 tsp vanilla extract

finely grated zest of 1 orange

finely grated zest of 1 lemon

3 large eggs

2 large egg yolks

1¹/₄ cups heavy cream

Preheat the oven to 350°F. Butter a 9-inch springform cake pan. Place a small saucepan over low heat, add the butter, and heat until melted, then remove from the heat, stir in the crackers and granulated sugar, and mix through.

Press the cracker mixture tightly into the bottom of the prepared pan. Place in the oven and bake for 10 minutes. Remove from the oven and let cool on a wire rack.

Increase the oven temperature to 400°F. With an electric mixer, beat the cheese until creamy, then gradually add the superfine sugar and flour and beat until smooth. Increase the speed and beat in the vanilla extract, orange zest and lemon zest, then beat in the eggs and egg yolks one at a time. Finally, beat in the cream. Stop the mixer and scrape down the sides of the bowl. It should be light and whippy—beat on a faster setting if you need to.

Pour the filling into the pan and smooth the top. Transfer to the preheated oven, and bake for 15 minutes, then reduce the temperature to 225°F and bake for an additional 30 minutes. Turn off the oven and let the cheesecake stand in it for 2 hours to cool and set. Cover and refrigerate overnight.

Slide a knife around the edge of the cake, then unfasten the pan, cut the cheesecake into slices, and serve.

tip Blueberry topping is traditional for New York cheesecakes—dissolve ¹/₄ cup superfine sugar with 2 tablespoons of water in a saucepan over low heat, then add 1³/₄ cups fresh blueberries, increase the heat, and cook until slightly softened. Remove from the heat. Meanwhile, mix 1 teaspoon of ground arrowroot with 2 tablespoons of water and stir into the blueberries. Return to low heat and cook until the juice thickens. Leave to cool, then spoon over the cheesecake and chill until ready to serve.

pies and desserts

banana cream pie

makes 8–10 servings

PREP TIME: about 30 minutes

COOK TIME: 25 minutes, plus 2 hours chilling time

1¼ cups all-purpose flour, plus more for dusting

12 oz prepared pie dough, thawed, if frozen

4 extra-large egg yolks

¾ cup superfine sugar

¼ cup cornstarch

pinch of salt

2 cups milk

1 tsp vanilla extract

3 bananas

½ tbsp lemon juice

1½ cups whipping cream, whipped with 3 tbsp confectioners' sugar, to decorate

Preheat the oven to 400°F. Very lightly flour a rolling pin and use to roll out the dough on a lightly floured counter to a 12-inch circle. Line a 9-inch pie plate with the dough, then trim the excess dough and prick the bottom all over with a fork. Line the pie dough with parchment paper and fill with dried beans.

Bake in the preheated oven for 15 minutes, or until the crust is a light golden color. Remove the paper and beans and prick the bottom again. Return to the oven and bake for an additional 5–10 minutes, until golden and dry. Transfer to a wire rack and let cool completely.

Meanwhile, put the egg yolks, sugar, cornstarch and salt into a bowl and beat until blended and pale in color. Beat in the milk and vanilla extract.

Pour the mixture into a heavy-bottom saucepan over medium-high heat and bring to a boil, stirring, until smooth and thick. Reduce the heat to low and simmer, stirring, for 2 minutes. Strain the mixture into a bowl and set aside to cool.

Slice the bananas, place in a bowl with the lemon juice, and toss. Arrange them in the cooled pie crust, then top with the custard and let chill in the refrigerator for at least 2 hours. Spread the whipped cream over the top and serve immediately.

chocolate-orange pots

makes 4 servings

PREP TIME: 10 minutes
COOK TIME: 15 minutes

1 orange

4½ oz semisweet chocolate, broken into pieces

2 tbsp unsalted butter

3 tbsp maple syrup

1 tbsp orange liqueur

½ cup sour cream

strips of orange zest, to decorate

Cut the peel and white pith from the orange and lift out the segments, catching the juices in a bowl. Cut the segments into small chunks.

Put the chocolate, butter, maple syrup and liqueur in a small pan with the reserved orange juices. Heat gently, stirring, until smooth.

Stir in half of the sour cream and the orange chunks.

Spoon the mixture into serving dishes, then top each with a spoonful of the remaining sour cream.

variation Top the pots with orange crème Chantilly instead of sour cream—whip ¼ cup heavy cream with 2 teaspoons of sugar and 1 teaspoon of Triple Sec until it holds soft peaks.

brown-sugar mocha-cream desserts

makes 4 servings

PREP TIME: about 15 minutes, plus chilling time

COOK TIME: no cooking

1¼ cups heavy cream

1 tsp vanilla extract

1¾ cups fresh whole-wheat breadcrumbs

½ cup dark brown sugar

1 tbsp instant-coffee granules

2 tbsp unsweetened cocoa

grated chocolate, to decorate (optional)

Whip together the cream and vanilla extract in a large bowl until thick and holding soft peaks.

Mix together the breadcrumbs, sugar, coffee and cocoa in a separate large bowl.

Layer the breadcrumb mixture with the whipped cream in serving glasses, finishing with a layer of whipped cream. Sprinkle with grated chocolate, if using.

Cover with plastic wrap and chill in the refrigerator for several hours, or overnight.

Remove from the refrigerator and serve.

variation Make the most of the coffee experience in these delicious desserts—replace the vanilla extract with 2 teaspoons of coffee liqueur.

pecan pie

makes 8 servings

PREP TIME: about 20 minutes, plus 30 minutes chilling time
COOK TIME: 50–55 minutes

Pie dough

1³/₄ cups all-purpose flour, plus extra for dusting

8 tbsp (1 stick) cold butter, cut into small pieces

2 tbsp superfine sugar

a little cold water

Filling

5 tbsp butter

¹/₂ cup light brown sugar

²/₃ cup light corn syrup

2 extra-large eggs, beaten

1 tsp vanilla extract

1 cup pecans, chopped

To make the pie dough, place the flour in a bowl and rub in the butter using your fingertips until it resembles fine breadcrumbs. Stir in the sugar and add enough cold water to mix to a firm dough. Wrap in plastic wrap and chill for 15 minutes, until firm enough to roll out.

Preheat the oven to 400°F. Roll out the dough on a lightly floured counter and use to line a 9-inch loose-bottom round tart pan. Prick the bottom with a fork. Chill for 15 minutes.

Place the tart pan on a baking sheet and line with a sheet of parchment paper and dried beans. Bake in the preheated oven for 10 minutes. Remove the paper and beans and bake for an additional 5 minutes. Reduce the oven temperature to 350°F.

To make the filling, place the butter, sugar and corn syrup in a saucepan and heat gently until melted. Remove from the heat and quickly beat in the eggs and vanilla extract. Stir in pecans.

Pour into the tart shell and bake for 35–40 minutes, until the filling is just set. Serve warm or cold.

mississippi mud pie

makes 8 servings

PREP TIME: about 40 minutes, plus 15 minutes chilling time

COOK TIME: 1 hour 10 minutes, plus chilling time

Pie crust

1½ cups all-purpose flour

2 tbsp unsweetened cocoa

8 tbsp (1 stick) cold unsalted butter, cut into small pieces

2 tbsp sugar

1–2 tbsp cold water

Filling

14 tbsp (1³/₄ stick) unsalted butter, room temperature

1³/₄ cups firmly packed dark brown sugar

4 large eggs, lightly beaten

¼ cup unsweetened cocoa, sifted

1 cup semisweet chocolate pieces

1¼ cups half-and-half

Decoration

2 cups heavy cream, whipped

chocolate flakes and curls

Preheat the oven to 375°F. Grease a 9-inch round tart pan.

To make the crust, sift the flour and cocoa into a mixing bowl. Rub in the butter with your fingertips until the mixture resembles fine breadcrumbs. Stir in the sugar and enough cold water to make a soft dough. Wrap the dough in plastic wrap and let chill in the refrigerator for 15 minutes.

Roll out the dough on a lightly floured surface and use to line the pan. Line with parchment paper and fill with pie weights. Bake for 15 minutes. Remove from the oven and take out the paper and weights. Bake the crust for an additional 10 minutes.

To make the filling, beat the butter and sugar together in a bowl and gradually beat in the eggs with the cocoa. Melt the chocolate in a heatproof bowl set over a saucepan of gently simmering water, then beat it into the mixture with the half-and-half.

Reduce the oven temperature to 325°F. Pour the filling into the pie crust and bake for 45 minutes, or until the filling has set gently.

Let the pie cool completely, then transfer it to a serving plate. Cover with the whipped cream. Decorate with chocolate flakes and curls and chill until ready to serve.

Buddy Valastro signature

This is a real favorite with my kids. The combination of rich chocolate cake, cookies and ice cream is a winner! Make the chocolate cake the day before if you want to save time.

chocolate cake

makes 2 cakes or 24 cupcakes

■ ■ ■

Buddy Valastro
Cake Boss

PREP TIME: 15 minutes
COOK TIME: 30 minutes

1 ½ cups cake flour, plus more for flouring the cake pans

1 ½ cups sugar, plus more for unmolding the cake

8 tbsp unsalted butter, softened at room temperature

⅓ cup unsweetened Dutch-process cocoa powder

1 tsp baking soda

¼ tsp baking powder

⅓ cup melted unsweetened Baker's chocolate

½ cup hot water

4 extra-large eggs, at room temperature

½ cup buttermik

unsalted butter, for greasing two cake pans

Position a rack in the center of the oven, and preheat the oven to 350°F.

Put the flour, sugar, butter, cocoa, baking soda and baking powder in the bowl of a stand mixer fitted with the paddle attachment. Mix on slow just until the ingredients are blended together, a few seconds, then raise the speed to low-medium and continue to mix until smooth, approximately 1 additional minute.

Stop the motor and pour in chocolate. Mix for 1 minute, then, with the motor running, pour in the hot water. Then add the eggs, one egg at a time, adding the next one after the previous one has been absorbed into the mixture. Stop the motor periodically and scrape the bowl from the bottom with a rubber spatula to integrate ingredients, and return the mixer to low-medium speed. After all the eggs are added, continue to mix for an additional minute to ensure all of the eggs have been thoroughly mixed in.

With the motor running, add the buttermilk, stopping the motor to scrape the sides and bottom. Continue to mix for another minute or until the mixture appears smooth. Before baking, be sure the batter is at 70–73°F or the cake will crown.

Grease two 9-inch cake pans with the butter, and flour them. Divide the batter evenly between the two cake pans, using a rubber spatula to scrape down the bowl and get as much batter as possible out. Bake until the cake begins to pull from the sides of the pan and is springy to the touch, 25 to 30 minutes.

Remove the cakes from the oven and leave to cool for at least 30 minutes, until they are room temperature, before removing from the pans.

chocolate-and-vanilla ice cream cake

makes 1 cake

PREP TIME: 10 minutes, plus freezing time

COOK TIME: no cooking

One gallon vanilla ice cream

One gallon chocolate ice cream

15 chocolate sandwich cookies, such as Oreos

1 9-inch round cake: ½ recipe of Buddy Valastro's Chocolate Cake (see recipe opposite)

whipped cream, for garnish

Remove ice cream from freezer to let it soften a little.

Place cookies in a large resealable plastic bag. With a rolling pin, smash the cookies until they form a coarse crumble.

In the bottom of a 9-inch springform pan, spread all of the vanilla ice cream. Sprinkle half of the cookie crumbs on top of the ice cream. Top that with chocolate ice cream, spread to cover the cookies and place back into the freezer to harden for about an hour.

To assemble the cake, with a serrated knife, cut through the chocolate cake so that you have two thin rounds of chocolate cake. Place the bottom of the cake onto a cake plate. Remove ice cream from the spring form pan and place the ice cream on top of the bottom layer of cake.

Place the other round of cake on top to make a giant ice-cream sandwich.

With a piping bag, pipe whipped cream onto the cake. Flatten it out with a large offset metal spatula.

Decorate with the rest of the cookie crumbs.

lemon meringue pie

makes 6–8 servings

PREP TIME: 30 minutes, plus 30 minutes chilling time

COOK TIME: 55 minutes

1 cup all-purpose flour, plus extra for dusting

6 tbsp cold butter, cut into small pieces, plus extra for greasing

1/3 cup confectioners' sugar, sifted

finely grated zest of 1/2 lemon

1/2 large egg yolk, beaten

1 1/2 tbsp milk

Filling

3 tbsp cornstarch

1 cup water

juice and grated zest of 2 lemons

1 cup superfine sugar

2 large eggs, separated

Sift the flour into a bowl. Rub in the butter with your fingertips until the mixture looks like fine breadcrumbs. Mix in the confectioners' sugar, lemon zest, egg yolk and milk.

Knead the dough briefly on a lightly floured work surface. Wrap in plastic wrap and chill in the refrigerator for 30 minutes.

Preheat the oven to 350°F. Grease an 8-inch round tart pan. Roll out the dough to 1/4-inch thick, then use it to line the pan.

Prick all over with a fork, line with parchment paper, and fill with dried beans. Bake in the preheated oven for 15 minutes.

Remove the crust from the oven and take out the paper and beans. Reduce the temperature to 300°F.

For the filling, mix the cornstarch with a little water to form a paste. Put the remaining water in a saucepan and add the cornstarch paste, lemon juice and zest. Bring to a boil, stirring. Cook for 2 minutes. Cool slightly.

Stir in 5 tbsp of the superfine sugar and the egg yolks, and pour the mixture into the crust.

Whisk the egg whites in a clean, grease-free bowl until stiff. Gradually whisk in the remaining superfine sugar and spread over the pie. Place on a baking sheet and bake for 40 minutes. Remove from the oven and cool.

Serve plain or decorate with whipped cream and fresh fruit.

apple pie

makes 6–8 servings

PREP TIME: about 45 minutes, plus 30 minutes chilling time
COOK TIME: 50 minutes

1 cup all-purpose flour
pinch of salt
6 tbsp cold butter, cut into pieces
1 cup cold lard, cut into small pieces
about 1–2 tbsp cold water
beaten egg or milk, for glazing

Filling
2 lbs apples, peeled, cored and sliced
²/₃ cup light brown sugar, plus extra for sprinkling
¹/₂–1 tsp ground cinnamon
about 1–2 tbsp water

Sift the flour and salt into a mixing bowl. Add the butter and lard, and rub in with your fingertips until the mixture resembles fine breadcrumbs. Add enough water to form a firm dough. Wrap in plastic wrap and chill for 30 minutes.

Preheat the oven to 425°F. Thinly roll out almost two-thirds of the dough and use to line a deep 9-inch pie plate.

For the filling, mix the apples with the sugar and cinnamon, and pack into the pie crust.

Roll out the remaining dough to form a lid. Dampen the edges of the pie rim with water and position the lid, pressing the edges firmly together. Trim and crimp the edges.

Use the pastry trimmings to cut out leaves or other shapes. Dampen and attach to the top of the pie.

Glaze the pie with beaten egg or milk, make 1 or 2 slits in the top and place the pie on a baking sheet.

Bake in the preheated oven for 20 minutes, then reduce the temperature to 350°F and bake for another 30 minutes, or until the crust is a light golden-brown.

Sprinkle with sugar and serve hot or cold.

pies and desserts

brownie cheesecake

makes 8–10 servings

PREP TIME: about 30 minutes

COOK TIME: about 1 hour 20 minutes, plus 4 hours chilling time

Base

8 tbsp (1 stick) unsalted butter

²/₃ cup semisweet chocolate pieces

1 cup sugar

2 large eggs, beaten

¹/₄ cup whole milk

1 cup all-purpose flour

Topping

2¹/₄ cups cream cheese, room temperature

²/₃ cup sugar

3 large eggs, beaten

1 tsp vanilla extract

¹/₂ cup plain yogurt

Decoration

melted chocolate, for drizzling

chocolate-dipped strawberries, to serve

Preheat the oven to 350°F.

Lightly grease and flour a 9-inch round springform cake pan.

To make the base, melt the butter and chocolate in a saucepan over low heat, stirring frequently, until smooth. Remove from the heat and beat in the sugar.

Add the eggs and milk, beating well. Stir in the flour, mixing just until blended. Spoon into the prepared pan, spreading evenly.

Bake in the preheated oven for 25 minutes. Remove from the oven and reduce the oven temperature to 325°F.

For the topping, beat together the cream cheese, sugar, eggs and vanilla extract until well blended. Stir in the yogurt, then pour into the pan. Bake for an additional 45–55 minutes, or until the center is almost set.

Run a knife around the edge of the cheesecake to loosen from the pan. Let cool before removing from the pan. Chill in the refrigerator for 4 hours or overnight before cutting into slices. Drizzle with melted chocolate and serve with chocolate-dipped strawberries.

strawberries with vanilla cream

makes 4 servings

PREP TIME: 10 minutes

COOK TIME: no cooking

1 lb strawberries, hulled

3 tbsp confectioners' sugar

1 tbsp lemon juice

1 vanilla bean

1 cup heavy cream

Halve the strawberries, place in a bowl, and sprinkle with 1 tbsp of the confectioners' sugar and the lemon juice. Let stand for a few minutes.

Cut the vanilla bean in half lengthwise and scrape out the seeds. Put the cream in a bowl and add the vanilla seeds and the remaining confectioners' sugar.

Beat the cream-and-vanilla mixture until it just holds its shape.

Divide the strawberries among four serving dishes, top with the vanilla cream, and serve.

variation Balsamic vinegar, vanilla and strawberries are a match made in heaven—replace the lemon juice with balsamic vinegar and prepare to be amazed!

raspberry-ripple ice cream

makes 6–8 servings

PREP TIME: 20 minutes, plus 30 minutes steeping time, 1 hour cooling time and 2–4 hours freezing time
COOK TIME: 25 minutes

1¼ cups milk

1 vanilla bean

1 cup superfine sugar or granulated sugar

3 large egg yolks

2½ cups fresh raspberries

⅓ cup water

1¼ cups heavy cream

Pour the milk into a heavy saucepan, add the vanilla bean and bring almost to a boil. Remove from the heat and let steep for 30 minutes. Put ⅓ cup of the sugar and the egg yolks in a large bowl and beat together until pale and the mixture leaves a trail when the beaters are lifted. Remove the vanilla bean from the milk, then slowly add the milk to the sugar mixture, stirring all the time with a wooden spoon.

Strain the mixture into the rinsed-out saucepan or a double boiler and cook over low heat for 10–15 minutes, stirring all the time, until the mixture thickens enough to coat the back of the wooden spoon. Do not let the mixture boil or it will curdle. Remove the custard from the heat and let cool for at least 1 hour, stirring from time to time to prevent a skin from forming.

Meanwhile, put the raspberries in a heavy saucepan with the remaining sugar and the water. Heat gently, stirring, until the sugar has dissolved, then simmer gently for 5 minutes, or until the raspberries are soft. Push the raspberries through a nylon strainer into a bowl to remove the seeds, then let the purée cool. Meanwhile, whip the cream until it holds its shape. Keep in the refrigerator until ready to use.

If using an ice-cream machine, fold the whipped cream into the cold custard, then churn the mixture in the machine following the manufacturer's directions. Just before the ice cream freezes, spread half into a freezer-proof container. Pour over half the raspberry puree then repeat the layers. Freeze for 1–2 hours, or until firm or required. Alternatively, fold the whipped cream into the mixture and freeze in a freezer-proof container, uncovered, for 1–2 hours, or until it begins to set around the edges. Turn the mixture into a bowl and stir with a fork until smooth. Spread half the mixture into another freezer-proof container. Pour over half the raspberry puree, then repeat the layers. Return to the container and freeze until completely frozen.

pies and desserts

INDEX